A Poke of Goodies

By

Joan Scher

ISBN-13: 978-1517157524
ISBN-10: 1517157528

This book is in a loving memory of my Mam.

CONTENTS

ACKNOWLEDGMENTS

My grateful thanks go to Mrs Jay Leffew. The book would never have been written without her. She has worked so hard correcting my misspelt words and dyslexia. So many thank you's Jay.

Also thank you to Mind in Bexley where I first joined their Creative Writing Group, and Mrs Margaret O'Neil as our leader who gave all of us members great encouragement. I do so appreciate their help and friendship.

The book is simply a collection of wonderful memories of many treasured friends.

Who first said blood is thicker than water? I have found in my life friends are thicker than water. Indeed friends are more precious than finding buried gold.

I began trying to write when I was 19. What I then wrote never interested anyone, until in the year 2000 I had become a member of Mind in Bexley's writing group, where I met Jay, and Margaret too who said, 'Please write down your memories,' which I have.

Joan

CHAPTER 1

Yorkshire folk

I wonder if Yorkshire folk, at least the women, will ever alter – well at least the true Yorkshire womenfolk? It was always known, when passing other folk's houses, that remarks would be passed.

"By gum, her windows fair sparkle, and t'steps are spotless."

"Aye, they say you can eat off t'floors."

"Her mother was t'same; not a speck anywhere."

"Aye, but at that end house – mucky rotten – t'windows are never clean." Points at the steps. "Never seen a drop o' water beyond t'rain."

"Nay, and ah 'ad to laff, she reckons to clean t'brass knob."

"Aye, brass knob, but what's under t'bed upstairs?"

"Nay I don't know."

"Hey, 'ave yer seen 'ow she 'angs t'washing out?" And so the discussion would go on.

Steps and flagstones would be swilled down every week, steps whitened with 'Donkey Brick', even round the drains and sinks in the back yards. If your nets weren't 'dipped' frequently you were a slut. Your little bit of front garden had to be tidy, no rubbish strewn about, and if kids chalked on the walls or flags they'd end up with a clout.

1

Nobody went shopping unless they wore a hat or headscarf, or hair was clean and tidy. To do otherwise wouldn't be heard of unless you were a mucky slut.

Your upstairs beds had to be made properly; sheets to be white as snow and hung out straight, 'blue bags' were dipped in the rinsing water to whiten them on washing day. Carpets had be taken up and beaten and the windows *had* to be washed, upstairs as well. Women had to open the casement, sit out on the window sill and close the window on themselves, to save falling off, then wash the windows. I was terrified when Mam did that. One poor woman had fallen and damaged her nose. It was partially removed and artificially replaced – I always remember how she looked, scared it might happen to Mam.

You also had to 'black lead' your fireside range and grates each week, polishing the tiles and hearth as well. A remark would be made if your shoes weren't shiny, although in poorer families, who couldn't afford shoe polish, it was excused, but you daren't go into Mam's house without taking your shoes off.

Poor kids wore torn trousers and 'hand-me-down' boots. Nowadays silly teenagers purposely wear these things thinking it's 'cool'. Little do they know what 'poor' really is.

Mam used to say, "Poor, maybe but you can still be clean." If you hadn't a penny to scratch your knees with you could still wash. Even pans off the fire had to be scrubbed and scalded before use again.

Back yards were filled with flowering plants in pots, but they still had to be swilled down and kept clean each week. Sadly, the people who moved in after Mam and Dad died, weren't clean. The next door neighbour took me upstairs in her house, to look out of her window and show me the back yard Mam had been so finicky about – it was like a rubbish tip; I couldn't believe my eyes, her lovely house a complete dump.

However, the clean will stay clean and typically 'Yorkshire' for always, it's in their blood. Mam used a peg inside the wash rag and poked in all the corners to, "remove muck; you don't want dirt in the corners, it breeds spiders and beetles." She found a 'Black Clock'* once, on our stairs; she couldn't sleep for nights worrying about a 'host' of them getting in.

"Where it's come from I can't say," she said, "probably the end house and it's travelled through yon muck." She would get hysterical if beetles, bats, mice, rats, pigeons, fleas and nits came near us. She would get Dad out of bed if she heard rubbing or scrabbling. "Don, there's rats, go down and get them." Then she'd lock the bedroom door behind him, as if any of them could climb up and turn the knob.

We never got these things (apart from one accidental visit from a rat, which will be mentioned later), she just worried. Oh well, that was Mam and her fear had its effect on me; I can't stand any insects.

Finally every *single* thing had to be ironed right, even dishcloths, dusters, lyle stockings, tea-towels, and bandages if there were any; no end of ironing. She even washed Dad's trousers if she saw them become shiny and once was so keen to iron them she ironed the creases down each side – Dad was furious; she never attempted that again.

Mam would tell me off if I ran about with some of the rougher kids. I remember once, when I had hit a girl I was playing with for being mean and spoilt, her mother started yelling at me. I was a bit scared so I ran home and told Aunt Winnie. She put her hat and coat on to march off around to the street, with me following excitedly behind. Knowing Aunt Winnie, there would be a battle ahead. When the woman saw her coming she turned scarlet

"Get your mucky windows washed, instead o' pickin' on bits o' bairns!" Aunt Winnie shouted. "Standin' on t'doorstep always gossiping!"

"Go on, give 'em it!" I added. Ee I was a 'bad little bugger', as Mam would have said. It was quite a row; I can't remember much after that, only that I never spoke to their kid again for years after. Trouble was I always did prefer playing with the rougher kids, they were more fun.

I wrote a poem about all that stickling for spotlessness – I fancied myself a bit of a poet when I was young:-

BE CLEAN

Everything in Yorkshire must be clean, clean, clean;
Anything mucky just hadn't to be seen.
You can allus have a bit o' soap to wash around yer ears
And to make sure you're washed for years and years and years.
Get yer mucky windows washed! Mek sure you're rid of slops;
Wash yer breeches regular, and don't be harbouring lops**;
Aye, polish front door knockers and sweep up under t'beds.
Keep your hair cut short, shampooed with never nits in t'head;

Your steps kept whitened, sinks as well; don't be a mucky slut
'Cos if you are don't visit me, my door to you is shut.

…And that is that…

*Cockroaches, black ones, and they made a clicking noise like a clock ticking.
**Fleas.

Great Grandfather and Grandmother Dickens with family
Thomas, Frances, Frederick, Nellie, Dora, Ada,
Oswald, Walter and Lucy   1880.

CHAPTER 2

Being Born – 1927

Somehow I can never believe my mother becoming pregnant, it always seemed most unlikely.

The intimate things of life were not discussed. Mam had to nurse Dad when he was very ill and she would whisper to me, "Ah just sponged your dad down, to keep him fresh – you know what ah mean…"

Yes, I knew, seemingly more about life than Mam ever did.

I had worked on a smallholding in Glaisdale during the Second World War; mixing with animals and farm lads soon knocked my innocence away; I learned fast.

Dad used to talk of the months before I was born and how nervous Mam was. "I had a bit of a carry on," he'd say, "when she was expecting you; it was a bit of a scream really. I did all of the shopping and walked your mam out during the evenings when, she would say, 'There's not so many folk about then.'

"She didn't want to be noticed even after you were born; I bathed you until she gained more confidence. It took a few weeks though."

When Mam actually went into labour she'd gone up the street, from our terrace, to Granny's house and told her. Gran said, "Aye, it will get worse."

The midwife, Nurse Prior, was a big woman and very abrupt. Mam began fretting. "Mrs Dickens, whatever is wrong? You're healthy enough, this should be an easy birth, try to calm down; it won't be born 'til midnight!"

This made my mam worse. The word 'midnight' did it. "Ooh ah hope not!" she wailed. "Born at midnight – that means the bairn will have second sight, if it's a girl anyway, ah don't want that!"

"Come on Mrs Dickens, that's a load of nonsense and Old Wives' tales!" Still, after a while, the nurse (who always called herself 'Nuss'), began to notice everything wasn't going quite as easily as it should. "Mr Dickens, can you get off to the surgery? I'll need Doctor Guy; nothing too bad but I'd appreciate t'doctor here." She gave Dad a scribbled note.

Dad set off and ran all the way down, past the Market Place and down towards the surgery, which was all locked up for the night of course. In his panic he dropped the letter, snatched it up and then noticed the flap was unstuck, so he read it:-

Dear Doctor Guy, can you come to this birth at 17 Tweed Street.
Mrs Amy Dickens is having some problem, thanking you.
By the way, these people can afford to pay.

Dad felt a bit huffy about this, hammering on the oak door. Eventually the doc appeared and cried, "Come on Donald, I'll give you a lift back; get in the car!"

His charge would be two shillings and sixpence (12½p), or maybe five shillings (25p) – a lot of money then. There were two other doctors, and all three were large, busy, bustling and loud. If Doctor Guy sat on a bed it sank considerably. He was a good doctor though, he could be trusted.

"Now Amy, what's going on here? Let me take a good look at you!" bawled Doctor Guy. (He always bawled, even at the surgery you could hear through the thick green baize door; all was revealed whenever a patient was being treated and given medical advice – no secrets there...)

"Oh Doctor Guy, do you think it'll be born at midnight?" Mother asked him. "If it is it'll have second sight!"

He cracked up with laughter. "Is that all that's worrying you? Be a good lass now."

Time went on and at last I was born, two minutes past two in the early hours of Sunday morning. Of course there would be no 'second sight'... Mam was more prone to have it than I was, as I found out in later years...

The result of my birth left her with a 'dropped womb'. There were no more babies. Mam wore a big pair of corsets for the rest of her life; 'Spirella', laced up over thin slivers of whalebone, with a wide flannel belt and pad for support.

I was born with strawberry marks all down my right leg and under my foot, some on my right hip, one on my face, which has faded now, and one on the back of my neck with a little mole in the middle of the strawberry shape. I had no end of remarks, from kids and grown-ups alike, along the lines of, "Eee, what've you done to your legs?" hence high polo-necks, and trousers or long woollen stockings on cold days. I had to wear 'lyle' types in warmer weather, never bare legs unless I used leg tan, which you couldn't get during the war years. I tried gravy browning but passing dogs found it rather tasty...

All through my young years I was 'mollycoddled'; always had to be well wrapped. I wore a vest and 'Liberty Bodice'; had knitted woolly socks, in awful fawn or beige wool, and massive scarves fastened with a safety pin. One scarf was more like a shawl (it had belonged to my granny), and woollen Pixie Hoods were knitted for me too because Mam said, "A vest for your back and a hood for your ears."

My chest was rubbed at night, with warmed Camphor Oil, and flannel bands went around my neck for bed – Mam's hands were rough, so I hated her rubbing my chest, and the flannel was prickly too. If anyone coughed or sneezed she would drag me out of their way. She once snatched me out of a seat on a bus because the man next to me had coughed.

I had to wear real leather lace-up brogues when all I wanted was black, patent leather ankle strap shoes with white socks, like a kid I played with; her name was Patty. Mam said, "You're not having daft patent leather, it's a good strong pair you need in proper leather, so don't start!" and she bought 'Kiltie' shoes for me.

She made all my summer dresses, and any spare material went into cutting out a pair of knickers big enough for a gust of wind to carry me off. The flowered knickers weren't so bad – I had to make do… It was a memory I put into a poem:

KNICKERS TO MATCH

Thinking back to when I was three,
Mother made frocks out of cotton for me;
Material left over would do for a patch,
But Mam used it up for knickers to match.

I didn't care for my home-made frocks,
Nor did I like her hand-knitted socks;
Knitted for me in fawn or grey.
Kids grinned at me as I went out to play.

When I was four came frocks galore;
Guess what came along too, more and more –
Knickers, yes, knickers, with elastic too;
The checks were the worst, in yellow and blue.
(Flowered knickers weren't so bad; I had to make do…)

When I was five and going on six
Mother again was up to her tricks.
'Cape Collars', frilled sleeves were in the next batch
And, yes, you're right – knickers to match.

When it came round to me being seven,
Thought there wouldn't be more; I'd grown up – thank heaven!
Looking back I feel quite sad;

I was luckier than others – I was warmly clad.

Still it went on, when I was eight,
I wasn't pleased so I didn't wait
To complain – my temper came up to scratch;
"Mam – I don't want my knickers to match!"

She took no notice. When I was nine
Lovely new frocks, it would be fine;
But with the frocks yet another batch
Of, yes, of course, more KNICKERS TO MATCH!

I resigned myself, when I was ten,
And I knew she'd started again.
Embarrassment began to hatch
Because left over bits became knickers to match.

The other kids were poorer than me;
There was no work for their fathers you see.
It was during the 'slump', long years ago.
I wish I could let my mother know;

I never said thanks for my home-made frocks,
And my toes were warm in those knitted socks.
My dad had work – a 'white collar' worker;
He worked long hours – never a shirker.

I was surprised, when I was eleven;
She didn't make them, I thought it was heaven.
Off I went to a boarding school;
A green and gold gymslip – but now the rule –
BOTTLE GREEN KNICKERS TO MATCH!

So, as I remember my childhood days,
I can only give them my thankful praise
For the home-made frocks and a bit to patch
That found its way for knickers to match.

Aged 4 taken
by Dad at
3 Glenfield
Terrace

in my
red
tin car

CHAPTER 3

Isabel

Mam was just three months pregnant with me when Mrs Codling, next door, gave birth to her only girl. She was christened Isabel.

She had six brothers, all of them dark haired as I remember, and mostly dark brown eyes – really good-looking and quite hefty lads.

After I was born it soon became clear that Isabel and I would grow up and toddle together. We played in our back yards together, but how I would have loved to also have six brothers, instead of being an only child.

Isabel was not spoiled. As soon as possible she was taught how to help around the house, learning to wash, cook, sew and mend, and to go to Sunday school and Chapel. I escaped all that. Her mam was a Primitive Methodist and sang hymns as she went about her daily work. She never raised her voice in anger, and I would think it was Mr Codling who would keep his sons in order. So Isabel was the seventh child; having a little lass was a delight to the Codlings.

When I was ill at fifteen years old, and sent away into the moor side village of Glaisdale, she came to visit. We would have long walks together over the moors. I never saw Isabel lose her temper, like I did. I was eight when I once pushed Isabel so hard, for being sarcastic to me; I banged her head against Mam's washing props on our back yard. As Isabel held her only doll its eyes fell out and Isabel cried. I have never forgiven myself for that. My dad put the eyes back but they didn't open and shut any more.

I had lovely dolls; a jointed doll, 'Mary', that had been Aunt Winnie's, and her big teddy bear with no ears, 'Betty'. There were 'Sheila Margaret', a large baby doll in lemon wool clothes, and 'Jean', which Granny and Aunt Winnie bought for me, second hand, for five shillings – 2/6d each, (12½p) which was a lot of money then, and a smaller teddy Granny bought me when I was one year old – I still have it, eighty-six years later, no longer yellow and fluffy.

I poked out his eyes and Dad sewed on tiny shoe buttons, which I removed and put in plastic eyes, fool that I was. I also had a stocking doll my great cousin Sarah made for me, dressed as a Scotsman, so he was called Sandy, along with Bobby Bear and Teddy Tail, until I realised Teddy Tail was a mouse and not a bear, but he is still Teddy. I had a lot of dolls, so you can believe what a horrid kid I was…

Isabel once spent sixpence on me, while she was away for a day, and brought back a doll's house set of dining room furniture; a little round table with roses on and four chairs to match. I said thank you and loved it, but spoiled it by saying, "Oh, she only spent sixpence…" My dad was so furious I didn't do that again.

Poor Isabel. She was much bigger than me, I was so skinny.

The last time I ever saw her was after I was married, and home for a visit, about the 1950s. She had become mentally ill, very seriously so, and in the York asylum – a hated word and heart-breaking for her family. I went to see her in York, with her mam. What a sad day to see her in a padded cell. Her mother was silently grieving. Isabel died about 1956. I was quite affected by her death.

I had noticed a change in Isabel before this but was never told how any of it came about, only that she had once had a serious fall off her pedal bike, while riding home from her uncle's farm where she often stayed, and had injured her head somewhat.

Isabel had written poems. I lost the notebook but found I had pasted three of them in my big family scrapbook, so I have a memorandum of her, and also one of my dolls wears a dress I made out of Isabel's favourite scarf, in red, pink, and cream stripes, which I had given her.

Her poor mam and I went to visit her and it was so upsetting to see Isabel. She came out with us into an open ward, for visiting, and she leapt over people's beds, like she used to down our front garden path at home; straight over three stone steps and our garden gate.

It was a very sad thing for me to see my old friend from childhood in such a mental state.

CHAPTER 4

Mam And Animals

Mam was never a dog-lover, nor pigs and horses after her fearful meeting with a horse on the way to the farm, and had ended up a nervous wreck, though the horse affair was hilarious.

It was a farm Mam would go to for eggs and butter amongst other supplies, where there were usually cattle in the offing but not all that evident. On this occasion however, a horse was not only apparent, wandering on the path, but noticing her with an aunt and cousin walking towards it. The aunt and cousin kept walking but Mam stopped and wanted to scare the horse away, so she pulled up sods of turf and flung them at the beast, "To frighten t'hoss away!" she yelled.

This, if she had thought about it, would have the opposite effect, because the horse began to come nearer in order to eat the grass she was 'offering'. Mam backed up and backed up, aunt and cousin now stopped to watch with grins on their faces, until she had backed all the way over the field and came up against a barbed wire fence.

In the meantime the farmer had come to meet them and became aware of the situation just as Mam got her dress so badly caught on the barbed wire it pulled it up so that her long bloomers were showing. The two other women were enjoying a real belly laugh by this time. "Noo then!" the farmer remarked. "What's tha' doin' holdin' on t'barbed wire with t'bloomers then?"

She then told me she had been attacked by a big old sow in the same field, then an Alsatian – "A great big dog jumped up at me from the back. I was terrified and just screamed." She told us so many tales about earwigs crawling into our ears, that bats would get into our hair, and even the harmless little whirligig beetles could get you as they scurried around on the surface of the ponds, etc., etc. These beetles often flew in through our open windows on summer nights.

She related that when she worked in Race's Bakery, in the market place, she found beetle legs in the flour used for the bread-making. She never got over it and stopped buying Race's bread.

Can you wonder I had problems as a youngster? I was always small in stature and it's funny the way dogs seem to like leaning on you when they like you. I used to find it a bit difficult (and on one occasion very painful, many years later having bunions, when a big dog stood on my foot and wouldn't get off). When I had three dogs, then grown up with my own family, it was a nightmare bringing them home when we were on holiday at Mam's; they were made to sleep under the wooden table in the scullery. It became almost impossible to bring them in the end.

How come I loved dogs so much, and cats and birds all my life, after living with my mam's foibles over practically everything alive?

Granny Robson loved Pomeranian dogs. There was Don who died before I was old enough to remember; quite a big breed of Pom, I was told. Aunty Winnie loved Don but Mam wasn't bothered much about him. She would never hurt a dog, but she really wasn't too fond of them.

Next came Dinky. He was so tiny, and such a happy little dog. We loved him as kiddies and loved taking him walkies. He wandered around and often stole into Granny's sitting room, or parlour as it was known, where he would lie on her curly black rug in front of the fire. Unfortunately he was curly and black too, so he often got stepped on and would yelp and snap at your ankles.

He didn't like Dad and would snarl at him when he came in through the front door. He would hang on to Dad's trouser bottoms, just a bundle of irritation.

My Friend Evelyn, up the street, had been pushing her little old pram and doll up and down the street when we both decided to dress Dinky in a doll's dress and bonnet and put him in the pram. Dad took a picture of this, which I still have, because he loved photographing unusual things.

Dinky was already old by this time and became ill. He was taken to the vet's and I think he had cancer. He was bandaged up and we were told he would get better, but he died when he was thirteen, poor little fellow.

Great Aunt Polly Bales had married Jim Bilham, and they lived at number fifteen Tweed Street. They were poor. Life, for them, was to live at the back of the house, in a big, dark kitchen with an inglenook, where a coal fire was permanently lit. They ate sparsely and at night they retired to cold bedrooms in the rest of the house.

Their children were Jack, Harold, May, Sarah, Daniel, Vera, and Margery. The Bilhams were so poor they went nowhere, only to their allotment garden up the lane. Jim would play his accordion in the evenings and Polly would sit quietly and listen. This was their entertainment. Polly always wore black and Jim liked bread spread with butter or marge, and would shake salt on it. As a kid I wanted to do the same but Mam wouldn't hear of it. "You don't eat stuff like that!" and neither could I eat any of the chutney the family made, because it was boiled in the old copper used for wash-days.

Jack was a black and white Cocker Spaniel. He belonged to my Great Cousin, Jack Bilham, and I never knew him, which was a pity because they said he was a wonderful dog. He came to live with them a bit before Jack and Harold went off to fight in the First World War.

Cousin Jack was in France and Aunt Polly was sitting in the inglenook one day when Jack the dog started barking frantically at the scullery door. The yard door swung open and who should appear, marching down from the top of the yard towards the house, but Jack in his full Army tackle.

Aunt Polly cried, "It's Jack!" Here was his dog bounding around desperately trying to get out then, as Jack bounded into the yard and Aunt Polly ran with arms outstretched, she saw her son disappear into thin air. The dog was running about looking for him, but there was nothing. That dear old dog knew there was something though.

Finally a telegram arrived announcing Jack Bilham was in hospital with shellshock. The family were shattered, and when he came home he was troubled for the rest of his life. We underestimate animals – they have a sixth sense.

Poor Aunt Polly; what a frightening experience, seeing her son walking down the yard, and his dog running to meet him, only for the man to disappear in front of their very eyes.

I never knew if he got better, or even married.

CHAPTER 5

A Goat Under The Settee

Mam always seemed to be going to farms for all kinds of produce – cheese, butter, eggs, curds and cream; she knew where to get the best stuff and there was a big farm up near the well-known 'Grinkle Park' of the area (a fine holiday hotel, which had been a family mansion belonging to the Palmers, who owned a large area of North Riding). The farm was well known for its splendid animals and clean barns, so Mam went quite unaware of the surprise in store for her.

She ended up sitting in a grubby sitting room, on a grubby sofa with the springs going, having a cup of tea – but she was in for a shock worse than the grubby surroundings as she looked around thinking, *Pity the house isn't as clean as the farmyard and barns are*, when she felt the sofa shudder. She nearly dropped her cup of tea. "Goodness and gracious to me! What's happening? Sofa's tipping up!" She looked for the farmer's wife.

The sofa heaved a bit more as something struggled to stand up in front of her, and there was a massive brown and white goat. "Hey, Missus, you've got a goat here under t'sofa!"

"Oh aye," came the answer. "It comes in to sleep there."

"By gum," cried Mam. "Ah couldn't cope wi' that! Ah noticed 'ow spotless your animal sheds are, why don't you mek t'ouse as clean? Mucky awd goat!"

Mam never went there again. She lost out on butter, which was still scarce even though the war was over by then.

CHAPTER 6

The Rat Through The Window

So many odd little episodes happened in my life, as in many other folks' lives, and often a great pity they were never written down.

I recall one autumn, for instance: The air was oppressive, as it so often can be at that time of year. I had been asleep in bed and could hardly breathe so pulled my old sash window halfway down. Almost instantly there was a downpour of rain splashing in over the open top ledge.

I was about to scramble out of bed to push the window back up when I yelled out. A rat, yes a rat, ran off the bathroom roof spouting and jumped onto the window ledge. I was very startled. How could a rat have been in our bathroom spout? The poor thing was half drowned and leapt down onto the floor then shot under my bed.

"Dad! Dad! There's a rat got in from the rain! Oh Dad – it's under the bed!"

"A rat? You fool, you're dreaming!"

"Nooo!" I yelled again. "No, it's under my bed – it's come in off the bathroom roof!"

Mam screamed, "You'd better go!" She leaped out of bed after Dad and locked herself in the bedroom. "I don't want it in here!" There she went, locking Dad out regardless.

Dad brought his leather slipper. He knelt down, pulled up the counterpane fringe, and wallop, bang wallop – bullseye!

Dad got it! The rat must've been paralysed with fright. What a shock for all of us, not least the rat, but especially for Mam who was trembling. Poor rat, I kind of felt sorry; it was only sheltering.

Mam touched my life in every way possible, whether she was there in person or not. She lived until ninety-eight years old.

Now, as I write this at the age of eighty-seven, I still dream of her; very vivid dreams, as if she is still alive.

Often I wake up perturbed.

One strange dream repeats itself: I am in my old home back yard; I am trying to push the outer yard door shut, so as to lock it and keep out whoever it is trying to get in. It's the same with the scullery door; I am banging the door shut and snapping the bolts across, turning the latch key.

Sometimes Dad is in the dream. Both he and Mam are there in the room and I know they are dead, but they are alive in the dream. It has gone on for nearly twenty years – strange – I don't know what it means…

CHAPTER 7

Remendies And Phobias

Mam kept worrying about everything to do with me; if I caught a cold, had swollen glands or a bad chest, she rubbed my chest with camphorated oil, then tied a piece of flannel soaked in oil around my neck. If I got earache she dropped warm olive oil into my ears and stuck cotton wool in them. When I caught German Measles she wrapped me up in a blanket after dabbing pink chamomile lotion on my sore spots; if the spots started weeping she dabbed iodine on each one. It stung.

Dad kept the iodine in an old-fashioned glass bottle, with a special stopper to dab it on with. I would scream as he dabbed it on. "For goodness sake!" Mam would say. "What a going on, it's only a drop of iodine!"

I ended up with a bad attack of whooping cough. Mam would listen to Old Wives' tales and one old woman told her to soak brown paper in vinegar and lay it on my chest, or smear my chest with goose fat. I can only think she got the goose grease from Grannie's goose at Christmas. There were wild garlic leaves in my shoes as well, which Dad had gone and gathered in the woods; they were put between paper and the soles inside my shoes. It didn't cure my whooping cough, just made my feet smell – just shows how much notice Mam should have taken of her advice.

Sore eyes, 'Pink Eyes', were always bathed in a solution of Borwick's powder, or I think bicarbonate of soda – *don't try it now*. I had anaemia so was dosed with Benger's Food or 'Compo', a strong pink liquid in milk. I took 'Virol and Robelene Malt Mix' for strong bones, 'Syrup of Figs' for constipation, 'Dolly Bags' for wasp stings, 'spirits of soap' for head lice, nits and 'dix' (another term for fleas).

There was 'coal tar soap', 'carbolic soap', 'salt plasters', onions, beef tea, and so it went on, remedy after remedy, and the old remedies worked all right.

Eventually the doctor told Mam I had septic tonsils and adenoids, so it was hospital for me. I was sent to a nice little private clinic, in Middlesboro', where the doctor was lovely. When he examined my nose and throat I actually screamed when he put an instrument up my nostrils.

He was startled and discovered my nose wasn't in the middle of my face; it wasn't straight. Nobody had ever mentioned it, consequently if anything was stuck up there it would hurt because there was a slight bend inside. The only time anything got stuck was when I pushed a bead up there; I can't recall why – the things children do, eh?

I fell in love with the doctor. I was eight years old. The nurses were lovely too.

I remember the chloroform mask being put over my face as I was told to count to a hundred; after ninety I was asleep. I woke up to a patch of blood on my pillow and noticed a kidney-shaped dish on the side trolley. I asked the nurse, "What is it?"

"To be sick in," she replied. I wasn't sick.

Later the nurse brought me a sweetened mug of tea and thin bread and butter, with apricot jam – my favourite jam. I managed to swallow it all.

I was kept in the clinic for over a week and could wander about freely. I was naturally nosey, so I tried all the doors; opened those that weren't locked and wandered in. One of them was the operating theatre.

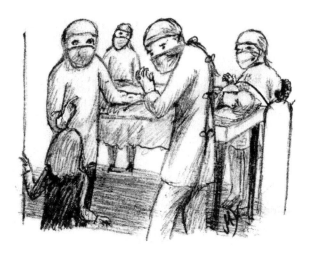

Why wasn't it locked? I was soon bundled out, but not before I'd seen the doctor doing something to a man's stomach, who was lying on a long table...!

How pleased I was, when the day arrived for me to go home, and I saw Dad's bowler hat bobbing down the road. I remember my Granny rushing down our garden path, arms open wide, "Oh, my bairn!"

Mam was nervous, even quite scared of so many things, for instance thunder storms frightened her an awful lot. She would call me downstairs if there was a sudden thunderclap and streaks of lightning flashed across the sky.

"Don't lie up there, we have a right storm threatening!" and she would light a candle or take a torch and we would sit under the stairs on a big old Victorian couch. First of all, though, she would open the front door, then the back scullery door, "To let the lightning through if it strikes down near t'door – it will go straight through and – will you come away from that window!" She would then draw the curtains. Of course the downpour would wet the scullery mat and the front vestibule but she must have thought it was worth the inconvenience.

I pondered over the lightning going *through* the house. How could a flash come in the scullery door, turn into the lobby, cross the kitchen out into the front passage, then go through the vestibule into the front garden…?

I was warned I must never shelter under a tree, or hold knives when it was streak flashes. Sheet lightning, of course, was safe and ripened the corn at harvest time.

If whirligigs flew in at night, attracted by a light we might have burning in a bedroom with a window open, they would fly up to the ceiling and whirl around up there.

"Don't go to sleep with your mouth open or they'll drop in," was Mam's advice.

Whirligigs are engaging little beetles and can be seen skimming and whirling across ponds, but I was always worried one *would* drop into my mouth. Mam believed earwigs actually crawled into your ears and bats would get tangled in your hair, which she often repeated to me.

Another thing; Mam didn't like me out in a gale – I was so thin she reckoned I'd be blown into the road and killed. "…And don't walk up near the houses – tiles can be blown off the roofs and hit you on the head." So I walked in the road! She was scared of just about everything. It's a wonder I'm not a nervous wreck. Poor Mam, her foibles seemed to get worse.

CHAPTER 8

Being Run Over

Joan.

Mam always used to worry about me running across the roads and getting run over; she never let me out on my own. What happened? I was run over when I was nine years old...

A girl I knew called Jean, who lived in the next street to us, once asked, "Do you want to come to the shops with me? It's only just down past Dam End." (This was the opening to where there was once a mill.)

I really wanted to go shopping with a big girl so I asked Mam. To my surprise she said, "Yes, but you hold on to Jean's hand tightly. Don't you let go, and mind you look left and right before crossing the road."

Jean was one of eleven children. Her ancestors were gypsy folk, now 'living in brick'. Mostly red-haired children, they were a happy, rowdy crowd.

Off we went. I felt so important going shopping with a friend older than me. Her dad wanted some nails from the little Ironmonger's shop. We carefully kept to the pavement leading us up to the market place and crossed over the road safely, walking down the hill a few yards to the shop.

After buying the nails, (24 nails for 6d – known as a tanner in the old money and the equivalent of 2½p today), we decided to stay on that side and walked down to 'Dam End', the road leading down to where the old mill once stood. There were no pavements when we reached the old stream, just fencing across the ditch.

The old stream still churned along, flooding over the road round to Espiners Wood. Opposite stood the old building which was a lemonade factory, still in full business when I was a kid. They made gorgeous lemonade, dandelion and burdock, orangeade and many others, much nicer than drinks today.

Here there was a blind corner, but the road seemed empty so Jean said we could cross. There was no warning; a large saloon car swung so sharply round the corner we both ran. I let go of Jean's hand and a big hot radiator came upon me like a monster's jaw. Next moment I was underneath doubled up. I remember to this day that oil was dripping and I was muttering, "I'm dead, I must be dead." Because Mam said I would be killed if I was ever run over.

A woman was screaming. I was in a daze as voices suddenly began shouting all at once; I heard feet scrunching all around; someone shouting, "Get the car off! Lift! Come on, lift!" I remember boots all around the edge, then the car juddered as it was bodily lifted by eight men, who had magically turned up to help.

I was so terrified I scrambled up yelling, "I want my mam!" and unconsciously dashed from under the car.

"Shock reaction; grab her!" I was duly grabbed.

"I thought it was our Audrey!" a woman was saying in obvious relief.

I was carried across to a little cottage and, amidst a number of folk churning around, deposited in a chair. A man was standing by, ashen white and shaking. He was the one driving.

I was being told to calm down and loudly scolded for running across the road in front of a car; then someone gave me a cup of tea, that spilled all over because I couldn't stop trembling and I couldn't hold the cup.

The man who had picked me up wasn't too kind at all; I hated him, and did for years after. I had just been knocked down and was scared, for goodness sake – I was only little for my age.

Finally I was carried out to the car. The driver was still shocked but it just happened he was a doctor, on his way to Scarborough for a Convention, poor bloke.

We drove up to the 'United Bus Garage', where a local policeman, P.C. Gregg, used to pop in for a cuppa and a gossip with the bus drivers. "We'll find him there," someone said.

When he was found and told what had happened, he came and put his head through the open car window. "If you ever do that again I will lock you up!" he told me.

No notes were taken, no report, no summons. They drove on to my house, and there were about four men in the car who lifted me out and carried me up the garden path, pushing the front door open. The gruff man, who had been bullying me, called, "Mrs Dickens, your lass has been knocked down. She's not dead."

Mam rushed out of the bathroom, where she'd been having a wash down, wearing only her pink vest and blue, long-legged bloomers. "Oh no!" she screamed. "I knew it! I shouldn't have let her out of my sight! What's happened?" She flew along the landing, throwing on her pinny and almost falling down the stairs.

I was laid in Dad's armchair, still dazed. Everyone was still talking at once. "Better send for t'doctor, Mrs."

"I haven't a phone, will one of you go along and phone for me, by the United Garage?" begged Mam. One of them agreed to do that and the rest of them left. We never heard anything from, or about, the driver again.

Doctor Guy rushed in, examined me, found no bones broken but there were a few sores, scrapes and bruises showing. "Keep her calm, put her in a deck-chair in your yard and give her ice cream to keep her cool." He left.

No ambulance was called; nothing else either, until, as Mam was 'sponging' me in a tin bath of warm water. The front door crashed open and Dad rushed in. "Where's our Joan? What's happened?" He saw me in the bath.

"A fine going on here," Mam said. "Look at these bruises!"

"I got off t'bus in t'market," Dad said, "and someone came up and told me, 'Don, your little lass has been knocked down at Dam End.' – I've ran all t' way here!" he gasped. He seemed to be the only one concerned. Not even my granny came down to see me, from up the street.

Jean was sent round to ask how I was and Mam shouted, "Clear off! It was your fault she was ran over!"

Jean ran up the yard, probably crying.

I had been wearing a pretty blue and white frock. It now had oil on it but Mam washed it and gave it to a little girl a few streets away, called June Cross. "You're not wearing that again – it's bad luck!" Mam snapped.

I wonder if the oil ever came out?

CHAPTER 9

Sledging

There was a sloping field which ran down past 17 Tweed Street, which belonged to Charlie Barker the butcher, and as kids we would build igloos and snowmen in the winter, sledging down the sides of the old pond there when it was frozen over.

Old Dick, Charlie's black horse, was often turned out there in the winter. He pulled Charlie's cart around. Charlie wasn't very keen when we ran about on his field, especially when the grass was growing. "Grass is dear," his wife would grumble at us, "we don't want it trampled on."

Joe, Charlie's helper, would break the ice when the pond froze, so old Dick could get a drink, and Granddad borrowed the horse and cart every now and then to carry peeled potatoes down to his and Granny's fish and chip shop. I went with him sometimes, but it was dangerous on the icy roads and old Dick's hooves would slip and slide as we went down Chapel Bank with the load on board.

In the winter of 1931-32 we had snow, snow, and more snow. My cousin had a very fast sledge, but I had a slow one which Granddad had made – I could go so far and then it would broadside and stop. We called it the 'Flying Tortoise'. My cousin's was the 'Flying Fish' because it was made out of old fish-boxes. Granny ran two fish 'n' chip shops (detailed in a later chapter), so there were plenty of smelly fish boxes about.

One day, when it had snowed really heavily, the local kids were going to a field to sledge. 'Gibbie's Field' we all called, it because it belonged to a local butcher called Gibson. It was a very steep field running down into a beck and *it was out of bounds to me.*

It had some quite dangerous 'sled routes' – one lad had recently broken his ankle there – but my cousin and friends persuaded me to go. I deliberately disobeyed my mother and went along, wearing a pair of bran-new wellingtons. (The term 'bran-new' comes from when delicate things were always packed in bran).

They persuaded me to sledge down the 'Snake Slope'. Like a fool I did and went at high speed straight into the slushy stream, all the muck and silt going over the top of my wellies. I crept home, dragging my sledge, the other kids laughing, and had to tell my mam. She was outraged. "How dare you deliberately disobey me!"

She took my sledge up the yard, got out the axe and chopped it up… oh! To disobey – it doesn't work!

Granddad shouted at Mam, "You didn't have to do that!" He tried to mend it but it was no good, it got burned on our fire in the end.

CHAPTER 10

'Snarla Ponds'

Old Alum works and mine, Hummersea.

Hummersea was about three miles away from Boulby Alum mines, where Alum was drawn through tunnels to the beach and boats waited to be stacked with the produce and shipped abroad. Probably the name came from the strange humming which came from the cliffs as the underground rail-track was in operation.

Snarla ponds were silent, overgrown and very, very deep. They were away over two different meadows, on the way past Street Houses, a tiny hamlet and leading out onto the road to Hummersea, taking you down onto the beach via the steep double cliff.

The alternative was to walk down to Loftus market place, up the North road and along by North Terrace where there was one shop. All kinds of goodies were stacked on the shelves and Mrs Lumb would weigh out all sorts of mixtures into paper 'pokes'. "A proper poke of goodies," she'd say. "Don't scoff 'em all at yance, you'll git belly ache!" My favourites and Mam's were toasted teacakes and liquorice sticks.

There were no shops if you went the Snarla ponds way. Dad and I would go for a walk around the ponds with a jar and net, picking out thick chickweed with tiny living creatures attached, then take them home and place a drop or two on a small glass slide to peer through Dad's microscope. It was so exciting to discover creatures not seen by just looking at the water; millions of insects we never see. I loved Dad's microscope; I still have it.

Mam used to lecture Dad about the ponds. "Watch our Joan or she'll be 'ead ovver 'eels under t'water!" she'd carry on. "There's too many folk drowned 'emselves in them ponds!"

In the end I got frightened of passing the ponds. It's true people did drown there, and they've now been filled in.

CHAPTER 11

A Handful...

I suffered from delayed shock after the car episode and developed a strange condition. I have never understood why I twitched and fell about so, and it seemed North Ormesby Hospital didn't know how to treat it either because I got no better in the three months I was there.

In the meantime I had very poor treatment from the Matron – she was a nasty woman. She would shout at me and I became hysterical, but she was never reported. (I wrote a letter home about her, which a sly nurse caught sight of. She sneaked the letter away and gave it to the Matron.) I was in a state by the time Mam and Dad took me home.

It was then decided I should live with a family of youngsters, out in the country, because the doctor said I needed to be amongst folk and not alone. Dad said, "Where can we send our Joan, if that's the case?"

"Now, how do I know?" Mam cried. "What *are* we going to do with her? They don't know what's wrong and I'm fair worn out with all her spasms and fits!"

They both talked to the doctor, and I never knew how they got to know the Hogarth family, in Whitby, but finally I was sent there, for over a year. I had to be kept occupied.

They were very good to me and kept a fairly large farm.

These were halcyon days (Kenneth Graham's 'Golden Age'). Messing about in the hayfields at harvest almost made me forget I was ill, and I got into trouble on many occasions, for instance when I found dressmaker's dummies upstairs, in a spare room at Airy Hill Farm, the Hogarth family's farm (mentioned again later).

I would pull these dummies out and pinch the daughters' clothes to dress them up, as a joke, but I overdid it. They looked on me as a handful and a bit of a nuisance – I think I'd had my tenth birthday by then – it was between the wars.

At the Christmas I was there I shook glitter all over the carpets. Aunt Aggie, the farmer's wife, was fed up with me but Mam and Dad were paying for me to be there.

I used to make piles of salt behind the chairs at home then sprinkle vinegar on them. If you asked me I couldn't tell you why I did these things, but the locals called me 'batchy' – a dialect word for 'just pain cracked'. Maybe so, I didn't know – it was fun though!

I used to hold the cow's tails at milking times, to stop the milkers getting swiped across the face as they sat on their three-legged stools, rhythmically squeezing the cow's teats – *sh, sh, sh, sh,* as the milk went into the buckets. I would get horribly sploshed when the cows dropped their plops – cow plops are not pleasant and I was laughed at – I hated that.

Ten years old seemed to be when I woke up to the charms of the opposite sex, because I 'fell in love' with Barney, the eldest son. He played the violin and was very kind and gentle; his younger brother, Tom, hated me and would hit me if he could.

Ted, christened Hedda, was the next youngest boy and was only five; I shared a big old feather bed with him, his little sister Millie and fifteen-year-old Winnie – a bit of a crush and Ted weed the bed some nights – my nightdress was soaked; it was awful.

41

Tom had the cheek to say, "You were always a nuisance," when he was older, and I'm sorry to say I eventually was, much to my embarrassment. It wasn't always me though, it was him a lot of the time. How I have wished to just be normal.

I met up with some of the family, years later when I was married. Whitby was a very historic seaside town, which I enjoyed. Always full of holiday makers.

Bram Stoker wrote his Dracula tales around Whitby and we did a 'Dracula Walk' one day when Victor, my husband, returned with me to live there in 1990. We were accompanied by Major Norma Richardson and Major Pat Charlesworth, of the Salvation Army, who had a great sense of humour. They were in fits of laughter a lot of the time and maybe that's why we didn't meet Count Dracula while on our walk.

These two Majors were responsible for reviving and reopening the Army Citadel there, after over thirty years of it being closed, and it's still surviving.

I also did a 'Ghost Walk' with my son-in-law Morgan. We toured East Whitby side and walked in and out of the yards and dark passages, finishing up in one of the pubs on Church Street, where the landlady of long ago haunted the premises.

It was very dark and 'old worldly' in the bar. We had our drinks and snacks in a very fitting atmosphere; it was packed with people in there. Then we got up to go. As we were leaving we had to walk through a passageway out and I spotted, on a wooden settle, a bulldog lying asleep. I think he was a French bulldog and I went over to him. He woke up and glared at me, with such an evil eye I had a really queer feeling and shuddered. I felt someone was behind me and left quickly. Was the old landlady lying there in the shape of a French bulldog? I didn't want to see.

There is 'something' about Whitby – they call it 't'awd spot'. You are warned, 'Don't ever criticize Whitby folks and the town, where you might be overheard!'

There are a lot of superstitions in Whitby; the 'Goths' would come there each year and take over the town, but they are welcomed by locals and have raised a lot of money for charities. Most of their people behave well, though there is sometimes a bit of unrest; they do look scary when there's hundreds of them all around town.

CHAPTER 12

The Grandfather Clock

In 1937 I would be just ten years old when the snow was on the ground. I sped up the street towards Grannie's house. Folk were digging away the melting snow from their doors and I slipped about on the slush. As I reached Grannie's door I grappled with the large knob, trying to pull myself up the step.

The door was still locked so I pulled myself up and turned the bell. It was a funny bell with a key-shaped handle and, as you turned it, it made a whirring kind of ring that almost made you fall over backwards, even if you were used to it. It was a relief to hear someone coming to open the door.

I was always scared of the front passage at Gran's. I never liked going to her house at, or after dusk, especially on my own. When I pushed open the front door, there on the wall was a fox's mask, with glittering glass eyes and a tooth poking out from its jaw. I daren't close the door behind me until I'd groped my way along to find the light switch, which was at the bottom of the stairs, and I'd hate to pass the old Grandfather clock, ticking slowly, 'tick – tock, **clunk**, tick – tock, **clunk**'; it was rather a loud '**clunk**' after every 'tock'. If it was near to striking the chains would whirr as the weight moved and the little door in the case slowly opened with the vibration. I didn't understand, when I was little, why it did that, and it terrified me because I thought something was coming out.

The coats along the wall, hanging on pegs in the gloom, didn't help. I'd brush into them and hats would often fall onto my head. I'd dash past, falling into the heavy net curtain which hung at the bottom of the stairs. (It was impolite, in those days, not to drape a curtain across; this was a private area.) I would imagine somebody hiding behind the curtain and grapple with the loose brass switch in desperation.

I could feel some kind of relief, when the light flickered on reluctantly, then flooded the passageway so I could return to close the front door safely and go flying through into the kitchen. Granddad was usually in his cane chair reading. He'd look up and shout, "What's going on? What are you rushing in like that for, and banging t'doors?"

I daren't tell him, or our Dennis, my cousin who always made fun of me, I was scared.

Gong back was even worse. I had to shut the kitchen door and switch the light on, open the front door, come back to switch the light off and dash out of the door, quickly banging it behind me, and running down the pavement to our house.

Sometimes when I stayed overnight, I would be awakened by loud snoring, like sawing wood, from Uncle Robert, and from Grandad snuffling and shunting sounds, like trains coming into a siding. When there was any silence between the 'sawing' and 'shunting' I could hear the old Grandfather clock ticking loudly and slowly, 'tick-tock-**clunk**', and how I wished I was in my own little bed, at home down the street.

One night I was staying there when a loud crash woke me in the early hours. Auntie Winnie screamed, "Rob! There's burglars, get up!"

Uncle Rob leapt out of bed, shook Granddad from shunting trains, and both rushed downstairs where they found the passage all lit up.

They searched everywhere but found no-one, and no sign of forced entry. That's when Uncle Rob noticed the little door in the Grandfather clock was open, and he shone his torch in. The weights had come loose and fallen off the chains.

"Why was t'light on then?" Granddad asked.

"That brass light switch is so loose any vibration flicks it on – it should be seen to," Uncle Rob said.

After Granny and Granddad both died, Auntie Winnie, who by now had left Tweed Street, offered me the Grandfather clock. I was married to Victor Scher by then, and he said, "Yes, we'll have it." I couldn't disappoint him so, with a struggle, Grandfather clock was carried out of the shop Aunt Winnie had taken over.

The case was strapped to the roof rack on our Morris Minor, and the face, clockwork and weights put in the back seat. We travelled all the way back to Uxbridge with it chittering and chattering as if it was angry. These were to be its last days in our family.

After suffering with the noise, and other drivers pointing and laughing at the old clock lying on our luggage rack, it was good to arrive home and set the clock in our bright little porch. Victor returned the workings, weights and chains to their rightful places, and the clock decided to go backwards. Unbelievably it was still going backwards weeks later.

Finally a young man noticed it and asked if he could buy it. He wouldn't be using the case, just the face and the inside workings. So off the old clock went on its last journey, to be completely changed. I was sad. That was one piece of Gran's furniture that finally left Yorkshire.

Uncle Rob in Granddad's allotment -1937 giving some idea of what the big old water tank looked like at the top of Rweed Street.

CHAPTER 13

Granddad Dropped A Trump

Granddad was always reading Zane Grey westerns. He loved cowboy stuff, and it was always Zane Grey as he sat in his cane chair.

One day Dennis was sitting at a nearby table drawing (he was good at drawing), and suddenly said, "Ugh!"

I said, "Aunt Winnie, Granddad's dropped a trump!"

"Not again," she said, "I've told him off once; it gets worse!" She went to a cupboard and took out a rag, one of several she kept for shining the grate with. She picked up the brass fireside shovel and put the rag on it, then with the brass tongs she picked out a glowing cinder from the fire and put it on the rag, which began to smoulder. She walked round and round with it making sure the smouldering would reach into the corners.

Granddad looked up and said, "What?"

"Aye," remarked Aunt Winnie, "you need say 'what'." But he just turned a page over and carried on reading.

Uncle Robert pushed open the lobby door, looked in and called out, "Summat's burning!"

"Aye." Dennis looked up from his drawing book. "Mam's doing her smouldering again."

"Oh heck!" and Uncle Robert shut the door. I heard him filling the kettle and then he opened the back door.

Suddenly the rag set alight on the shovel and up sprang a flame, so Aunt Winnie chucked it onto the fire quickly. We were all coughing and choking by this time.

Uncle Rob was rattling cups. *Ooo*, I thought. *They're going to have tea.*

"You'd better get, *cough, cough,* down 'ome, *cough,* your mam will, *cough, cough, cough,* 'ave your tea ready, *cough,* our Joan..."

I was hoping to have stopped there for tea, now the smoke was beginning to clear, in spite of Granddad. Then Uncle Robert came into the room. "Smells like Ol' Nick 'as passed through!"

"Who's Old Nick?" I asked.

Our Dennis sneered. "Oh, our Joan doesn't know who Old Nick is!"

Well I didn't; I had never heard of him. When I got home Mam had done bread and butter and pineapple chunks. I was sick of pineapple chunks every Sunday. I wasn't happy.

Dad looked up from reading 'The Times' as I walked in (Mam always read 'The News of the World'). "You're down early," cried Mam.

"Yes, Granddad dropped a trump and so..."

"Now then," scolded Dad, "we don't want to hear anything about that!"

Oh well, I thought, *another Sunday nearly gone.*

CHAPTER 14

Scary Corners

Apart from the dark passage in Gran's house, with the frightening fox mask, 'something' behind the curtain and the strange old clock with its 'tick-tock, clunk', there were other episodes which frightened me.

Whenever I had a sleep over at Gran's I was put in the box room. I didn't like the box room, with its sloping ceilings – who had slept in it? Could it have been Emily Griffiths, the grandmother I never knew? On the walls were hung Bible texts, and one awful framed sepia photograph of a horrible accident in a moor village, where a farmer, with his Shire horses pulling his wagon over a small bridge, had suddenly lost control of the Shires and they had reared up. It was known as 'Beggar's Bridge', which spans the river Esk.

One poor beast had gone over the edge and was hanging by its reins, and the other poor thing had been crushed against the bridge wall so badly that it had to be shot. The first, once cut free, had been able to swim out of the river, terribly scared and trembling.

How long they had been in that state before help was possible goodness knows, but it was long enough for photographers to turn up and take their pictures. These dreadful photographs, when developed, sold like 'ripe cherries' all over the North. I couldn't bear to look at the one in that box room and always averted my eyes.

There was also an enormous white wooden trunk, which

took up half the space in there, and under the bed, box after box of old curios were crammed together, including stolen bird's eggs. Mam's long golden plait of hair was there as well and I would have loved to have it, but I was not allowed to look at anything, and Mam's plait was thrown away. All I have of Mam's now are her picture postcards, her Japanese fan and a paper parasol from when she was a little girl.

Another thing I found very frightening was the need to go to the lavatory during the dark hours. A wee wasn't so bad because you could use the potty, but anything else and there was the chill of a night time grope for a torch, unlocking the scullery door and walking all the way up a large yard until you arrived at a passageway to the earth closet. There you had to find the matches and light a candle.

Aunt Winnie would come with me when I was younger, but it was still very creepy, and as I got older I was left to cope alone. Sitting out there, with a candle casting weird shadows and a door which opened outwards, wasn't much fun, especially on a cold night dressed only in pyjamas and a coat! I am claustrophobic; so is Mam. Maybe it's because, when we were naughty as children, Gran had a habit of shutting us in cupboards by way of punishment.

Mam used to be shut in the linen closet upstairs, screaming and shouting and banging on the door to be let out. At least when I was shut in the cupboard under the stairs I was with my cousin Dennis. We'd start playing together happily enough, but then he'd start trying to be boss, I'd argue and we'd end up fighting.

Granny would whip us round our chins with a wet dishcloth and then shut us up under the stairs, which smelt horrible. All the family's shoes and wellies were kept in there, and we'd be in there 'til we promised to behave. A crack in the door served as a peephole and we'd press an eye to it to see what was going on and who was passing by the door.

Granny Robson.

Granny's younger sister, Edie, seemed to take against my mam and was for ever telling tales on her, so Mam used to be shut in the linen cupboard upstairs for punishment. Mam, named Edith Amy, Edith after her Aunt Edie, would scream. She suffered with claustrophobia for the rest of her life because of this. She didn't like rooms packed full of people, or low ceilings and attic rooms – they made her panic.

Just once I was shut under the stairs alone, for breaking something. I felt stifled, as though I couldn't get my breath; it was really scary.

When we were let out again Granny would warn us, "Now, if there's a wrong word, as big as a hayseed, I'll come across wi' me dish clout again!" but we still all loved Granny, for all that.

I would be eleven when my Granny died. I was shaken and it left an empty hole in my life. Nothing was the same. Mam went hysterical, Aunt Winnie morose, and none of us accepted her death easily; she was only sixty-two – it was unbelievable.

Mam sent me away to a farm up at Grinkle because I wasn't allowed to attend 'fewndrals'. I think possibly the farmer's wife had been at school with my mam; she was a jolly woman who tried to cheer me up and I think I had the most lovely, fresh and tasty lunch ever that first day.

An egg, so fresh it was still warm from the chicken, boiled just nicely, and her own home-made farm bread and farm butter, just churned, white and rather salty. Afterwards a gorgeous apple pie with a beautiful short crust, and the perfectly cooked apple was from her own tree. What a feast; it couldn't be faulted, only Grannie's death spoiled the atmosphere.

When I went home I didn't go to Grannie's house until the next day – it was dead; it felt claustrophobic. There were cakes left over, in her walk-in pantry, from the funeral.

"Choose one," Aunt Winnie said, but I didn't really want it.

Granny Robson and Aunt Edie.

CHAPTER 15

Budgie

Before this I was in Newcastle Infirmary for four weeks and then was taken to Riding Mills Convalescent Home. It was 1939 and while I was there war was declared. All the children convalescing there had to be brought home.

I had been away for three months without Mam and Dad visiting once. The only visitors were Dad's cousins, living in Ponteland, and I didn't really know them. While I was there I had my eleventh birthday and Mam and Dad actually bought me a green budgerigar. They taught it to say, "Where's Joan?" What an amazing thing for them to do.

I was in the children's ward and the nurses were kind enough. I seemed to have a nervous condition which caused me to feel fear a lot of the time. One older girl, in an end bed, used to sleepwalk, which I hadn't heard of, so it upset me that she would wander about at night; on one occasion she was fiddling about around my bed and I was quite frightened of her.

Also the large wall-clock did not tick in a calming way; it gave one single, loud, sharp tick every minute. I couldn't stand it. I was crying. The kindly ward sister decided I was better off out of the ward because of the sleepwalking girl, but then I was told I would be going into the women's ward, I kept on crying.

Sister Brown then asked to have my bed moved onto the shaded veranda and at last I was able to be more relaxed. It was strange at first. Sister Brown came and sang to me:

I'm so happy, here's the reason why,
Jesus took my burden all away.
Once my heart was laden with a load of sin,
But Jesus took my burden and my heart within.
Yes, I'm so happy, here's the reason why,
Jesus took my burden all away.

She had the most lovely, kind brown eyes and I knew then that she was a Christian lady. If only she could have known how those words stayed with me; I still sing them loudly when I'm feeling 'down'.

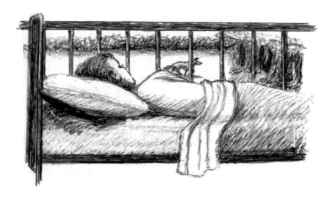

I was able to sleep at night and could stare out at the beautiful countryside. I saw my first fox walking in the early dawn.

A few days later we were all to be evacuated and Dad arrived in the car. He hired the chauffeur and car from the steel-works to take me home where, waiting on a large stand, in a cage, was a green budgerigar – our little Budgie; it had been a most wonderful birthday gift. He stayed with us until I was fourteen.

Over the years Mam worshipped little Budgie; she taught him to say 'Budgie, Budgie, Budgie' and 'Pussy cat, Pussy cat where have you *been?* – I've been...' After 'been' he would never say any more of the nursery rhyme.

Aunt Winnie, her sister, loved birds and dogs but never cats. I caught Mam once, during one bad winter, feeding an old tatty cat that had been abandoned, and actually boiling potato peelings for the wild birds. She'd throw them up onto the coal-house roof, which was covered in birds. No telling, with Mam, what would come next, but the variety of birds was wonderful, despite seagulls gate-crashing in on the feasts.

CHAPTER 16

Uncle Joe, My Hero

Youngsters often have a hero and mine was Uncle Joe; a biggish man with gingery hair and a reddish face (although he was almost bald as far as his hair went). He lodged down the road, in Arlington Terrace, with an old widow woman. He only had one sister, who lived in Whitby. We never met her.

He and Dad were very close friends and keen readers, sharing books. They were also both watercolourists (painters Mam said, she wouldn't have known the word 'colourist'.)

Their pictures were excellent, and over the years local folk would have a watercolour, or a black and white pen-and-ink drawing off them. I have kept a number of lovely pictures and am very proud to have them.

Uncle Joe never married, nor even had a girlfriend. As Mam said, "He's never had a woman." Like my dad, he was a mathematician and worked over at the furnaces, originally 'Pease and Partners' and then 'Skinningrove Iron and Steel Company'. He was an accountant, along with Dad, five miles away in Skinningrove; a queer little village, tucked under the cliffs the other side of Hummersea – a strange and wonderful cove with the amazing double cliffs leading round to Boulby. It was so rough and dangerous it was never a place for folk to visit or spend a day swimming; the North and East coast was and is quite risky.

Uncle Joe and Dad, along with other fellows, joined up with our family and we would traipse our way to Hummersea for a dip; a little less dangerous than Boulby. When the tide was out many folk would walk to Skinningrove. Uncle Joe and Dad loved hiking but Mam never went.

They would sit either side of our coal fire, Dad on the left and Uncle Joe on the right, while Mam did the ironing with one of the most dangerous inventions you could imagine. A gas iron which was plugged into a gas-tap, normally situated in the floor next to a wall, with a long, flexible tube, and she had to light it with a match inside the iron itself.

Amy ironing with a gas iron, East Loftus, 1940.

Every Christmas and birthday Uncle Joe would buy me poetry books or 'Pooh' books. 'Christopher Robin' was a great favourite. I love the books and still have them in my bookcase, with his lovely writing, dated from 1933.

He and Dad, one year, made me a most wonderful doll's house with real little framed pictures, carpets and many carved bits and pieces. How I treasured that house, with little windows that opened.

I played with it proudly 'til I was twelve, when Mam said it was 'in the way'. She gave it to a family at the end of our street, who eventually burned it under their copper; how sad is that?

Uncle Joe had a twitch in his eye. I often wondered how many women imagined he was fancying them. He was invited to all Granny's Christmas parties, and three spinster sisters, Mam's friends, purposely played a very silly game of 'winky'. Each man in the room would wink at a woman sitting in the room who, with screams of laughter, would rush over and sit on his knee.

Poor Uncle Joe came in for some 'stick'.

If we ever said he fancied Mam, who was bonny with cornflower blue eyes and hair the colour of ripe corn, he would laugh and say, "Gerraway, don't be so daft!"

I would be about seven when Uncle Joe never came again. He left his lodgings and went back to Whitby, I never knew why. Had he and Dad quarrelled, or what? I would be fourteen before I ever saw him again, on a bus. He looked at me queerly, as if he didn't recognise me. I remember it well (I realised later I must have looked very different after seven years).

As time went by I was eventually told that Uncle Joe had 'taken his life' in a tragic manner; I was still not told how. Gone was my favourite hero of my infant life. His sister was still living at the time, but I never knew her.

CHAPTER 17

Christnas at Number 16

Christmastime, and New Year, bring back the most wonderful and happy memories for me, at least while my amazing Granny was alive.

She opened her house up for big celebrations, when family and friends were invited. Her real name was Sarah Ann Bales but she was known as Sally 'Ropson' (Robson), and you were indeed honoured to go to one of her 'do's'.

The decorations went up on Christmas Eve morning. An old paper frill hung across the kitchen ceiling, holly behind pictures on the wall and paper-chains everywhere. There was an artificial tree ablaze with blown glass ornaments, angel's bells, robins and all sorts of things, with real candles, each set in their own little metal clip-on candle-holder. ('A real tree meks so much mess wi' all t'needles prickin' into your clothes an' all over t'carpets.' Granny would say.)

The good carpets, in the kitchen and parlour, were taken up some days before and the winter carpets went down. It was a ritual. They had to be hung in Charlie Barker's field, out in the 'backs', where Aunt Winnie would beat them to get the dust out, before putting them away until it was summer again. The thick, black curly rug in front of the fire had to be removed for two reasons; in case toffees, nut shells and other bits and pieces were trampled in, but also because black and curly Dinky got trodden on.

The carpets were slung between four posts, with thick

ropes. Charlie let my Gran hang all her sheets and washing there as well. Charlie was the local butcher. Granddad gave him a hand in the slaughterhouse, across the main road from our house. It broke my heart to hear the pigs screaming – animals know when they're going to die. I would block my ears and go into the scullery so I couldn't hear.

My Auntie Winnie, with Uncle Robert and their son Dennis, who lived with Gran, had the job of beating the carpets using wooden bats. Dennis and I loved having the bats to whack the carpets with. All this was done days before it was time to prepare the feast. So much food, I often wondered where it all came from; the eating just went on and on until after New Year's Day.

There was a large walk in pantry, with a large marble table top. Shelves lined all the walls, top to bottom, and it fascinated me to walk in and see jar after jar of jams, pickles and other preserves, as well as the china and rows of pans. There was a safe for meats and other perishables, because there was no fridge.

Granny did most of the baking with an old gas cooker in

the scullery, and a large range with a side oven and a boiler with a brass tap, in the big kitchen.

*

The Christmas cake was made in October, wrapped in greaseproof paper and put in an airtight tin with an apple, "To keep t'cake moist," Gran would say.

I have never seen such a large Christmas cake since, nor have I tasted one better. It was a most gorgeous cake, and so beautifully decorated.

That too was Aunt Winnie's job. Two days before Christmas the cake was put on a great glass dish; she smoothed on thick golden marzipan and finished the fancy edges with a pastry tool. There was no white icing – decorations went straight onto the marzipan; crystallised lemon and orange slices all round, then gold and silver balls, red cherries, walnuts and in the middle a tiny robin which bobbed up and down on a little spring. A china Father Christmas was placed alongside him, and finally a broad paper frill encircled the whole cake.

There was just one more thing needed, the Cake Cover Doll. She was a small celluloid doll, with painted eyes, wearing a voluminous, frilly, orange crépe paper dress and she was placed carefully over the cake, "To keep the dust off," Auntie Winnie would say. It was a work of art indeed.

Great Aunts Jane and Edie then appeared, with Mam, to give a hand with preparing for the twelve days of feasting.

Both Christmas Day and New Year's Day meant goose, turkey, chicken, beef, and a large ham. The roasting smells were so mouth-watering.

Granddad always kept a pig on his allotment; Auntie Winnie kept chickens, but the goose, turkey, and beef came from one of the local farmers.

There the Christmas pudding, made months earlier and laced regularly with spirit; it would have silver threepenny pieces secreted inside on the day, along with silver thimbles. Besides all this there would be mince pies, tins of choice red salmon for dozens and dozens of sandwiches in the evenings, and jugs of thick fresh cream from the Great Cousins, John and Harry Pybus, who had their own milk business.

Johnny, as he was known, came every day. He was a very small man, sitting in his cream milk cart with his churns, being drawn along by a patient old brown horse.

Johnny wasn't a patient man; you had to be ready with your jugs and basins for him to fill, so one day, when Granny had forgotten to have the container ready early, he came along and noticed the freshly cleaned chamber pots (pittle pots) sitting on the bottom of the stairs, ready to be taken back up to their various rooms.

"Where's t'jugs?" he called out. "I ain't tahm t'wait!" and he promptly filled the potties with the required amount of milk.

Granny threatened to kill him.

After a big Christmas Day feast there'd be home-made wines, all kept in a little dark cupboard. Dad opened a bottle of bramble wine Gran had left in the cupboard for about three years. As the top came off it shot out in a fizz, straight up to the ceiling, and cascaded back over the snow white table cloth, down Dad's suit and splashing Mam, who was sitting next to him on the 'bit of good settee'.

There was a drop of the wine saved. "By gum, strong stuff that was…" according to Dad, but imagine poor Gran's face at the mess.

New Year's Eve arrived and what a spread again. Thirty guests were arriving and the big table was spread with goodies. There were bowls of whipped up frothy jellies; red, green, yellow and orange, and more jugs of fresh cream, plus tinned peaches and pears.

There were snowball cakes, rolled in jam then sprinkled

with desiccated coconut, butterfly cakes, gingerbreads, rich rice cakes, chocolate cakes, sponge cakes, apple slab, more mince pies and sandwiches galore, all made by Granny. What a great supper. There were bowls of fruit and nuts and sweets standing here and there as well.

After this the fun began; polkas in the kitchen, singing songs in the parlour, with either Mam or cousin Alfie on the piano. There was Dad with his violin, Uncle Rob on his ukulele and we blew bazookas, or combs covered in greaseproof paper. Then there would be games of Charades, and the old game of 'Murder', where everybody spread out around the house; upstairs too. The murderer was secret, of course.

One party night the murderer was Edward Brown, a friend, and he 'murdered' Dad on the top of the stairs. Crash! They both fell down the whole flight and knocked over the old Grandfather clock at the bottom.

What a commotion! Luckily they were only bruised and the clock survived intact. Wonderful memories of fun, singing and music, laughter and happy faces always linger in my mind.

I remember one Christmas I awoke at about five o'clock on Christmas morning and jumped out of bed but, seeing an empty pillowcase at the end of my bed, just lying over the brass rail, filled me with dread. Santa Claus had not come after all. What an awful feeling; my stomach sank to my feet.

I rushed out of the bedroom shouting for Dad. He came rushing out of his room to find out what had happened but, as I ran along the landing, I fell into a large, bulky bolster case, crammed full of parcels. Santa had left my sack on the landing; a pillowcase had not been big enough. *What* a relief and *what* a mammoth Christmas stocking!

"What a lucky little girl you are indeed," said Dad, but Mam was a bit crotchety at being woken up so early. I couldn't wait to run up to Grannie's and tell her about the sweets and puzzles, games, books and dolls, and oh, so many delights in that sack.

On another Christmas I was in the kitchen when Johnny bustled in. He'd stopped to tap the barometer in the passage. "What's the weather going to do today, Johnny?" we'd always ask, and he always got it right.

Then Granny turned to him and asked, "Aren't you ever goin' to give our bairns a bit of sommat for Christmas? All these years an' you never 'ave!"

Johnny replied by tossing two threepenny bits, the yellow metal ones, on the table, crying out, "Christmas should nobbut come yance in three yer, then it wad be ovver many tahms!"

"Miserable awd beggar!" Granny chipped out.

Poor Johnny – years later he drowned himself in a pond on their farm. He never smiled as long as I'd known him.

CHAPTER 18

A Grim Tale

I never thought I would ever tell these tales about my family, I have so many happy and amusing memories which I keep in my head, but now I feel they deserve to be aired; nasty ones too, for instance Granddad Robson. We always thought he was extra stressed at Grannie's passing, for years. Although the letter Grannie had kept talking about never appeared, Granddad saw the bank manager alone and then came back to declare, "It's all mine, all left to me!"

None of the family really believed the boast, and weren't impressed when he became a drunkard and just wasted it on odd women. He eventually brought one of them home and married her.

The family was disgusted at his behaviour. Before Granddad 'the old fool' had found this 'second wife' (such as she was) he had, one Sunday afternoon, been sitting in the front parlour when he rushed out, calling to Aunt Winnie, "I've just seen your mam!" He was white as a sheet and trembling, "She's come back!" he gasped.

Aunt Winnie, quite fed up, replied, "Serves you right, you old bugger – she's come to haunt you!"

His marriage to the second wife lasted all of six weeks, when the new bride cleared off with the wedding gifts and was never heard of again.

In the end he became a real handful for Aunt Winnie and Uncle Robert; she decided they should move out of number

17 and make a life of their own, with the little dog they had by now, named Wong, but the old man decided to sell up and move with them. Aunt Winnie had adopted a daughter, two-year-old Lois, who had grown up and also had a baby girl by this time – unmarried.

They moved into town, where they took a small shop premises and put Granddad in a downstairs room.

Peter came along, for us, after Granny died. He was a bright, excitable dog. When we wanted to put his collar on he became impossibly excited and would twirl round and round and would cock his leg at every upright when we took him out. Consequently it took a bit of time to complete a walk with him. We had him for some years before he passed on and we found ourselves with a handsome Chow Chow named Chang.

I was surprised to see Chang had a black tongue, but evidently this was his particular breed, with a beautiful, rich sienna brown and gold coat. He lived for fourteen years until one day he disappeared. Uncle Robert was the most distressed, though of course we were all upset wondering where he'd gone. Two days later he was discovered lying under a hedge, away up in the fields, dead. He must have gone there to die.

By the time this took place Dennis was married and so was I.

The next alarming episode came about a year or so later.

Everyone was asleep, after a busy day in March, when Lois suddenly awakened, fighting for breath. "Gas! Oh Hell it's a gas leak!" She flew about waking everyone up and pushing open all the windows, then she rushed downstairs unlocking all the doors. She was in hysterics as she searched for the leak, terrified of an explosion.

She fell over Granddad's body, lying with the gas tap in his mouth. He had covered his head with a clip mat off the floor and was, of course, dead, but it was sheer luck he didn't take all their lives with him.

There had to be an ambulance and police; Lois had grabbed baby Kate and now they were all outside, shivering in their night clothes, hardly able to take in what was happening.

As usual I wasn't told 'til it was nearly over, after the post mortem, so I didn't attend the funeral, I now can't understand why. I never could get my head around all these secrets, nor could Mam it would seem. She seemed to think I shouldn't be told these things, but I could cope with life better than any of the family would ever know.

CHAPTER 19

Another Grim Tale

After all this was over Mam told me other things, going back to when the Second World War was on. I was home from weekly boarding school and she said I was protected when a bomb was dropped in the field opposite our house. She revealed that Granny had appeared to her and she got out of bed to tell me, "There's a German plane hanging about and I want you downstairs." I obeyed and went into the kitchen, sitting in Dad's big chair in front of the back window. "Get out of that chair and under the stairs!"

She lifted up a big old sofa in there and shoved me under, just as a bomb screamed down, shattering windows and ceilings. Dad rushed in yelling, "A bomb! Get down, get down!" and ran back out again because he was a warden and had to be on duty.

The budgie was flying around in the darkness, because the blast had knocked its cage over and burst it open. As we were groping around I came across the cage on my way to the scullery, where Mam was trying to sort things out, and I was surprised to feel the budgie flutter into my hands. "Budgie's in me hands!" I yelled. "He's flown to me!" Funny, no-one ever gave him a proper name, he was always just 'Budgie'.

Meantime Granddad had come rushing down the street shining his torch all over the place to see what had happened. Someone shouted, "Get that torch out!" but he carried on until he got to our house.

The budgie was put back in his cage and was eventually hung back up where he belonged, but two weeks later he was dead and I came home to find Mam, with the cage on her knee, crying her heart out over him.

So, once again Mam had had a 'warning'. I try to keep all these happenings at bay in my mind, but I have to accept that Granny had come back each time for a reason, and it wasn't for me to question what Mam said about it. Granny had been there for me at the right time, because it was my bed that had been covered in large chunks of debris, and Dad's chair one mass of broken glass. Thanks Gran! I pray one day, when I leave this life, she will be there waiting with her arms open wide to greet me and give me a hug. There is no doubt she saved me that day.

Dad thought I was injured and carried me out in my pyjamas, to a waiting car, and we went to my cousin Emiline where I stayed for a few days.

I missed Granny so much. A big empty hole was left.

She had such a great sense of humour; nothing in number 17 ever felt the same again. There were no big parties or comings and goings, as there used to be. There was no-one to give us half oranges with sugar lumps soaking in the juice.

Granddad was still alive, but he didn't spit pips into the

fire anymore, because Aunty Winnie wouldn't have any "Mucky carry on!"

I only once went back to where Granny was buried and had a little weep at her graveside. I felt comforted then, somehow. What a great lady, and friend.

CHAPTER 20

'The House That Jack Built'

Great Aunts Betsy and Nellie, Clarence, Donald and Alice.

I was eighteen before I discovered some of the history of Gran and Granddad's house. I'd known nothing of it up 'til then, but Dennis was helping me to scrape the paper off the kitchen walls and there it was, 'Jack Griffiths, 1888'. It was just one of three houses he'd built.

Jack had been an iron foundry worker in Wales and he and his family had come to England, to find work following the railways as they were being built. They decided to stay in the North. As their family grew Jack Griffiths found work easily, despite him and his wife being unable to read or write. It was a tough time for Great Granny, always giving birth and up and moving so many times, but they lived reasonably well.

One son, William, turned out to be a scholar, and later younger son Jack (named after his dad) became a wealthy young man, owning a clothing warehouse. Sadly four youngsters died as infants.

Thomas was the third born but was illiterate. He didn't do very well, having a weakness for beer, but when he married his family did quite well it seemed. I was to meet up, quite late in life, with one of his sons; a very gentle person, and intelligent.

The girls, five in all, followed their parents and ended up living in East Loftus, County Cleveland.

Great Granddad went on to become a master builder. He and his sons were very practical and built three fine houses, one being number 17 Tweed Street, which they moved into soon after building it. A few years after building the three houses, he was to be employed in an iron ore drift mine; attached to the Iron and Steel works 'Pease and Partners' owned by Quakers, in Skinningrove. He ended up as overseer to 70 workers and the pit ponies there. Illiteracy was no object to a practical and talented man like Jack.

Dennis outside number 17.

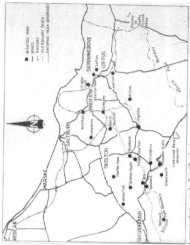

Location of mines in the East Cleveland area. There were six ironstone seams in East Cleveland and these varied considerably in quality and thickness. The Main Seam was worked by almost all of the productive mines. Known as 'Blue Billy', it was fourteen feet thick in places and yielded ore with the greatest iron content. At Loftus mine the Main Seam was nine feet thick and split by a band of poor quality ironstone or 'dogger'. Safety at the mines was paramount and matches and cigarettes were not allowed below ground, but in latter years ordinarily miners hid cigarettes in packets of Polo mints so they could smoke in the drifts, an action which could have cost them their lives.

The Waddle Fan engine house at Loftus Mine at present houses a display area for the Tom Leonard Mining Museum. In the past the Waddle Fan, built in Wales by the Waddle Patent Fan Co., was used to extract air from the mine via the brick lined drift. The steam engine, and later an engine powered by electricity, was situated in the engine house. The fan itself was on the back exterior wall...

SKINNINGROVE MINES

Skinningrove (Loftus) Mine. Skinningrove valley was one of the first sites of ironstone mines in East Cleveland, although at first it was limited in scale. Greater access by the opening of the railway in 1866 allowed J.W. Pease and Co. to commence mining in the hillside by digging drifts (tunnels) into the East side of the valley beneath the town of Loftus. By 1895 Pease was supplying Skinningrove Iron Co. with 9,000 tons of ironstone per week. By 1900 an interlocking grid of drifts from Whitecliffe, Grinkle and Skinningrove brought ironstone to the surface at Skinningrove, crossing the mine site on this wooden bridge, entering a drift on the other side of the valley and being drawn up for transportation to County Durham. If readers wish to learn more about ironstone mining, Tom Leonard Mining Museum is a good place to start.

Donald and Clarence Stalker with Great Aunt Nellie.

He and his wife, Emily, had three sons, William, John and Thomas, and five daughters, Betsy, Nellie, Alice, Annie, and Emily. After some years of the family being together Betsy and Nellie married local lads and went on to start up their own homes. Unfortunately Betsy had married a lad considered to be 'beneath the Griffith family' so they were practically ignored. I had seen them in town but wasn't told who they were.

William emigrated to America; Great Grandma went to live with Nellie and her husband in Liverton; their son,

Clarence, became director of a coal mine in Ponteland so they did very well, some of the richest of the Griffith's ancestors.

Edith Amy Robson, 6 months.

Winnie aged 2 years.

Winnifred Mary Robson, aged 6 months.

The youngest daughters, Alice, Annie and Emily stayed home to look after their parents. A little while after that Jack died. His death caused a rift, I never found out the reason, and the family split up. Alice and Annie sold number 17 and went to set up their own business, taking on a small hat shop, until Annie died. I vaguely remember her; a sweet, delicate woman.

Aunt Alice never married and ended up a 'business woman' in town, with a double fronted shop; a fine Ladies' and Children's outfitters; millinery and drapery.

For some strange reason Emily went to live in Lancashire with her brother, John. She eventually met and married a young man, a tailor named Thomas Dickens (the 'waster' mentioned earlier). They had two sons, Donald and Edward. Donald Dickens was to become my father. All of Thomas's siblings did quite well, girls too, despite a lack of education.

The Dickens family were very gifted in art, singing, and music generally and the girls all made their own clothes.

Great Granddad was a singer and choirmaster and led his own brass band. Mam said he was 'a big man in the Methodist chapel'. He sounds like someone I would have liked to meet, in fact I would have loved to have known the whole family but never did see much of them. Great Granddad Dickens died when he was seventy-eight, a sad loss to everyone.

When Emily, very sadly, contracted T.B. and died, Donald stayed living with his father, but Edward was sent to live with his Aunt Nellie. Then when Granddad Dickens became ill, Tom and Donald moved to Yorkshire.

Number 17 was bought by another family, who Granny then became friendly with, and four years later they sold the house back to Gran and Granddad, who were still a young couple at the time, when Mam was their only child.

Auntie Winnie was born at number 17. There would have been seven of them, but Gran, very sadly, had five miscarriages and only Auntie Winnie and Mam were lucky enough to survive. Granny herself had been a 'blue baby' – how amazing she hadn't died at birth.

It was to be many years later that Auntie Winnie and her husband, Robert Harrison, produced the next birth, in the form of my cousin Dennis. I was born to Mam and her husband, Donald, three months later.

Donald at seventeen.

Donald Dickens was seventeen when he was out walking with his dad one day and noticed my mam cleaning the windows of the baker's shop. She was eighteen by this time, and Donald told his father he liked what he saw, and he meant to make her his wife. Donald was an office boy and was with his firm for forty-eight years until he retired. (They asked him back after a while because they wanted to know the price of the new blast furnace that had been installed, and he stayed on for another two years before he was able to retire finally.)

He was soon courting Mam. Calling at number 17, and being invited in, he had no idea he was entering his own grandfather's old house, and that his mother, Emily, had lived there as a little girl. How strange for us all when we finally discovered the truth of it. He and my mam were married in that house, where the small family reception was also held, and four years later I was born in 'The House that Jack Built'. Great Granddad Dickens, according to my mam, was a very kind man. She got to know him after meeting Dad because they went to Lancashire, where he lived, on visits.

Amy and Donald, married at Loftus methodist church.

Great Granddad Dickens.

Granddad (Tom) Dickens - 1900.

Great Grandma Dickens.

CHAPTER 21

Married In Haste

Aunt Winnie and her husband lived with Granny and Granddad at the same time, because Aunt Winnie had 'fallen' to a pregnancy – Dennis, my cousin.

When Aunt Winnie had 'got herself into trouble', Granny Robson 'did her nut'. Aunt Winnie was only nineteen and she sobbed a lot. She was really a lovely person; extremely kind-hearted.

Granddad tried to protect her, but Granny cried out, "Leave this to me, Ben! She's fetched shame here! Our Amy behaved herself all the years she courted with Donald. Now Ben, tek this lass, and our Amy and yon lad, down to a little chapel somewhere. I'll buy both of 'em a new frock and a pair of shoes each!"

Granny wouldn't attend the wedding but at least she let the unfortunate pair move in with her to live. I grew up feeling sorry for Aunt Winnie. Her new husband, Uncle Robert, had come from a fisherman's family, in a small village nearby, where you could walk along the cliffs, at one time, to get to the Staithes; it was a bit treacherous in parts though.

Once they were married Uncle Robert and Aunt Winnie had the small front room at home and never had any place of their own until they were retired. All Uncle Robert earned in those early days was 6d an hour, filling trucks with iron ore from Liverton mines. Eventually, when Granny expanded her fish and chips to another outlet, he took charge of the second one and they all lived fairly happily together.

Mam and Dad had a good life, in comparison. Having lived their sixty-nine years in a terraced house, they moved into quite a nice old folks' home in Saltburn. It broke their hearts having to leave their home after a lifetime.

Victor and I had a notion to buy number 17 after we were married, but Mam didn't seem keen so we never did – too many bad memories.

CHAPTER 22

Fish 'N' Chips

Today folks wouldn't believe the fish shop Granddad and Uncle Robert built for Granny. What a pity no-one ever took a photo of it. It was a lean-to, built onto the end of the house in Tweed Street. No permission needed in those days, they just laid a concrete floor; brick walls built up from this to about three feet high; wooden walls next, lined with asbestos, topped off with tin sheeting which was finished off with tarmac.

The large fryers were arranged at one end and a fire was lit under them. Having been pristine clean, in green and cream, it wasn't long before they were grimy with smoke and fat, and piles of newspapers were left about for wrapping the fish and chips in. On one occasion a pile came in with a bit of old closet forgotten inside.

Every fire risk right there before your eyes, yet it never burned down. What is more the old stable, belonging to Joe, was just at the end of the fish shop passage – no health restrictions either; there it was for many years, long after Granny died – I haven't tasted fish and chips as good as Granny and Granddad's since.

You could buy scraps, in a greaseproof bag, for an imperial penny, with loads of vinegar which we could suck out of the corners of the bag – oh, delectable!

Fish was 3d (thruppence) a piece; maybe 4d if it was larger, and a hay'p'ny (halfpenny) or a penny for a portion of chips.

Although married in haste, Aunt Winnie and Uncle Robert were happy together. Though Dennis was their only natural child, Aunt Winnie had always wanted a girl and that's why Lois was adopted as a two-year-old.

I remember going with Aunt Winnie to North Allerton to collect Lois. She was being brought up by two very elderly spinster aunts. They must have been so upset when their little niece was taken from them. It was thought that she, once she was grown up, would take up the fish shop business but she became a nurse instead. Lois brought up three girls, in later years.

It may be that her mother was a Matron and couldn't keep her but, as always, I never was told Lois' full story. I do remember, though, for a long time she would call us 'My dear gel', which must have come from her aunts, even at that early age. She died when she was only fifty-nine, having been born with a heart problem; two of her daughters also died prematurely, at forty and fifty-four, Julie from severe M.S. and poor Kate with a tumour on the brain; so very sad. Carol, the eldest, moved to Scotland with her husband and family, and I've neither heard nor seen anything of them since.

Uncle Robert developed diabetes. I can remember he once went into a coma, as he was driving his motorbike and side-car, and drove into the local cemetery wall – he told me, "Aye, well, ah crashed into t'right wall! Ah couldn't've found a better place if a'd kicked t'bucket!" luckily he was just badly shaken and not severely injured. I was very fond of him.

Aunty Winnie loved dogs and poultry and I used to feed her hens. Once one of her cockerels followed her out of the run and ran all the way to the post box with her and back. Folk thought it was a great joke. All creatures seemed to like her.

However, she hated cats, and so did Dennis – when he was about two months old, in his pram in the back yard, Aunt Winnie heard a choking noise. She flew out to his pram to find the next door neighbour's cat lying on his face.

Granddad had a tame seagull he called Jack. How old he was I can't remember but he came for years. The butcher's wife used to grumble because Granddad threw fish bits for Jack and the hens would eat them. The eggs she gathered and sold ended up tasting fishy.

CHAPTER 23

My First Jobs

It's always a bit scary, starting your first job, and my first was unpaid, at the age of fifteen.

During the war I was sent to live in the beautiful village of Glaisdale, over the Whitby moors, with a middle aged couple who had never had their own children. The initial contact was a little unnerving.

I was sitting in our front garden, doing a watercolour of the fields and bushes opposite, when a strange man opened the garden gate and, without speaking, slowly walked up the garden path. He seemed as if he was weighing me up, and so it turned out he was. This man was to become Uncle Walter, to me, and his wife Aunty Betty – as usual I hadn't been duly warned about this, but I was expected to go and live with them.

I was introduced properly, then given the once over, and two weeks later I was saying "Cheerio," to my friends and family, dressed in my new red coat, complete with suitcase. I found myself with Dad on the little 'Bluebell' moor bus, travelling away on a most wonderful scenic journey, to spend the next four years with this couple. I was made very welcome.

I had 'passed muster', and what an interesting life it turned out to be. Uncle Walter was an architect, but it also turned out he enjoyed watercolour painting, so we became very involved in art. He taught me many things about painting – the old school style.

Aunt Betty was an elegant lady; well spoken, and always wore a pretty housecoat whenever we had visitors. She would never be seen in old clothes or aprons. She was a great cook and, even though it was during the war, I remember we had such rich food. They kept rabbits, hens and a pig so we were never short of food.

They were going to look after me but, in return, I would help around their smallholding, which I loved. My first task was to feed the twenty-five hens and collect eggs. Uncle Walter showed me the trap nests where the hens laid their eggs and how they had learned to climb in through a flap at the back of each wooden box.

I couldn't understand why there was a need for this flap, because when it dropped behind them they were trapped until they were let out. I think this was cruel. My first time collecting and releasing the birds was fine but, as time went on, I would often forget and the poor things would miss food and water.

There was an occasion when I received a terrible shock on opening one of these nests. The hen had been in there all night and had been attacked by a rat. The rats ran about quite freely (there was a gap they could get through, just a couple of inches at the back of each box). I wanted to be sick because the poor thing had no head left, what had it suffered?

Another experience was with an old broody hen, who was sitting on an egg, and when I opened the flap she pecked me, straight up one of my nostrils. Gosh how it bled but, thank God, it wasn't my eye.

I also had care of the rabbits; feeding and watering of course. They were in two houses with various rabbits in separate cages; I also had to clean their cages out, and was lucky enough to be there when a Belgian Hare, named Priscilla, gave birth. It was so interesting but, knowing no better, I went to touch the litter I had seen – only to find their remains the next morning.

I was frantic, Priscilla had completely eaten about five of them; I was told she believed they would be 'safe inside her again', which is a 'thick trick'. Are rabbits that stupid?

There came a day when I was shown how to kill a chicken for dinner. I was expected to kill a cockerel and I pulled too hard. Its head came off and it ran about, flapping and headless. I was terrified – blood everywhere.

One morning I went to feed Emma, the pig, and discovered one of the hens had managed to fly over the high wire netting into the pigsty, which had evidently frightened Emma so much she had slipped and injured herself. I was told to rub liniment into her sore spot for weeks. It wasn't until she came to be slaughtered that the man who came to do 'the pig killing' told us she had a broken rib and must have been in pain with it.

She was hung up and the blood drained from her into a tin bath, out in the field. I had the task of stirring the blood over a paraffin stove, to keep it from congealing, so Aunt Betty could make black puddings. I never eat black pudding…! One year she put sugar into the mix, by mistake, instead of salt. The puddings were inedible. Aunt cried at the waste of food.

Uncle Walter had the task of curing the hams and sides with alum and saltpetre, down in the cellar. We were able to keep one ham and one side, the rest went to the meat market and Uncle shared the offal with villagers.

Poor old Emma; I was really attached to her. I remember mostly the task of picking ticks off her and putting them in a jar of Pyrethrum powder to kill them. She was always so pleased to be rid of them.

CHAPTER 24

Saving Fishes

I had many weird adventures in Glaisdale; there were many interesting characters living way out on the moors. Uncle Walter knew a lot of them and so I got to meet them. Aunt Betty had a niece, Dorothy, who had a happy disposition and was an attractive young woman. We got on well together, but she was rather an excitable person.

We all used to go off walking and, one Sunday, having wandered through Mill Wood (where I'd spend hours gathering mosses, wild flowers, nuts, and fir cones), we came to an old stone style, made by monks in days gone by. (As they went they laid sandstone paths as well, carrying the slabs with them and placing them as they walked.) We climbed up the flag steps and over the wall. Here there was a tiny ditch, where Marsh Marigolds grew in profusion, known locally as King Cups.

We could pick wild flowers in those days and I would gather Bluebells, wild garlic and Red Campion to take home to Aunt, along with the King Cups.

After we had crossed the style we looked back at the old water wheel and mill cottage. People still lived there, but I think mainly 'townies' who had plenty of money and bought up these marvellous old places as their summer retreats.

How I wished I had photos of all this, to copy into paintings.

We clambered on down by the old stone wall to 'Boddy's'

fields, belonging to a strange farmer – I was uncomfortable in his presence. The River Esk ran through his fields, and near a hedge there was always a small pond, which may have some water trickling from a spring. On this day, however, it was really hot, and everything was drying up. What had been a pond was now like bubbling mud, alive with all the fish struggling to survive. I couldn't leave them like that so I gathered up thick handfuls of mud and rushed over to the river, slinging the fish into the fresh water, which was still running quite swiftly.

Dorothy was running behind me, shrieking, as I put my hands in the mud and she saw the fish wriggling, while Aunt and Uncle were roaring with laughter. After about six or seven attempts it seemed I had scooped out all the fish – I didn't see any frogs, but then they would have hopped to safety anyway I suppose. Dorothy had kept on running backwards and forwards, at each of my handfuls of wriggling fish, and long before I was finished I was filthy, so we returned home.

If anybody had been about they must surely have thought we were very strange, but at least the fish would survive. There were good salmon in the Esk.

I had another episode in 'Boddy's' fields, when I was there picking Celandines. The wildflowers in Glaisdale were just so lovely; many species I had never seen before. I was there on my own when something suddenly snapped across my shoe. It was a rabbit 'snatcher' – catgut set on a spring, which could have caught many other creatures; moles, voles, mice, etc. I was enraged, so I ran madly about pulling them all out and slinging them into the river. Old Boddy must've been mystified, wondering where all his 'snatchers' had gone. I didn't go to Boddy's fields again after that.

CHAPTER 25

The Summer House

Every year, on Aunt's birthday in July, she and I would pack sandwiches, and the last of her strawberries, and walk towards the station, then, at a certain point, cross the line and wander down the embankment to the river's edge. There was a flat rock in the water and a little gap where the water collected itself into an 'almost pool' full of minnows.

We used the stone as a seat, and also a picnic table, and we would dangle our feet in the water to be tickled by the minnows. Oh, it was so peaceful. I gathered Monkey flowers (Wild Balsam in bright yellow and russet brown), violets, and clumps of lovely moss, with which I made miniature gardens, in bowls. They were marvellous times for Aunt and me.

Aunt Betty's birthday was on Saint Swithin's Day. Luckily I don't remember it ever raining that day, so we didn't get the forty days of rain that the saying promised.

I can see all of this time so clearly in my mind.

Uncle Walter had an old summer house out in his field. He'd built it years ago. There was an old table, a stool and a desk, old tools, rope, and an old corn cracking machine, used for cracking maize, which was still in use. Uncle's fishing lines were in there too, because he liked to go trout fishing, and Aunt would be waiting to cook them for our supper. So delicious. I tried my hand at fishing, but it wasn't my thing.

Uncle let me tidy up the summer house and hang pictures up, and I also brought my paints and books etc. there to enjoy. I spent many hours in there painting, and decorating jars and pots as well. I was able to invite friends too, it was great fun. The hens would wander in, and sometimes sit on the desk, and I had a tame little cockerel I called Percy – I can't remember if we ate him or not...

In summer the grass in the field grew so long it became a hayfield. Uncle had a lad come along to cut it and then it was baled, just raked into small heaps when it was dry. That was a good time.

It reminded me of when I was younger, back before the Second World War when I was living at Airy Hill Farm in Whitby, with the grand family Hogarths. I'd had an exciting life there and harvest time was fascinating. Building up the haycocks was fun, and laughter and excited screams filled the air, but we five kids really had to do some sensible work, then we got to ride on the hay carts, pulled by massive shire horses.

There were thermoses filled with cold tea and a nip of Epsom Salts to make it more refreshing, and Aunt Aggie, as I knew the farmer's wife, supplied her own gorgeous home-made plum pies. There were beef sandwiches in home-made, crusty bread, with farm churned butter. Oh, halcyon days. It wasn't quite the same here, with Uncle Walter, but it was good.

Uncle was very 'short grained' (short tempered). He would teach me how to mix colours, and I learned a lot, but one day I wouldn't listen to him because he was angry, so he broke my paint brushes in half. Another time, when he was enraged at my cockiness, he shouted and I slung all my paint pots into the grass. He said, "They'll stay there until t'hay is cut!" I said I didn't care.

Oh yes, we often had rows, but never Aunt and me, she was too elegant and gentle.

I did care about my pots, of course; luckily none of them had broken.

Uncle, being artistic and musical (he was a cellist and often played his cello in the evenings) would put on pantomimes each winter. He was intellectual and wrote his own scripts, arranged the music and invited the whole village to take part, teaching them dance routines and giving them singing lessons, so he had duettists and soloists as well as a choir, temperamental though he may be.

He made and painted the scenery while Auntie made all the curtains and some costumes, and rehearsals began in September. It was quite exciting, but I was too nervous to take part in any acting at that time. By the time performances came round the village hall was packed out for every show.

My dad was invited to perform his magic, and also to join in the music with his violin; Aunt and Mam could both play the piano as well, along with the village string band. We had wonderful shows, as good as any professionals. Oh what glorious days – I never seemed to miss Mam and Dad, nor my friends back home, nor them me it would seem. It was a new life and more exciting.

At last I plucked up courage, at his performances, to do a walk-on part but I got stage fright and was quietly led off. The audience didn't know. Years later, I finally became a part time performer and ran my own entertainment group, around North Yorkshire, just an amateur effort but it was well received. However that's another tale, long after I was married and Uncle Walter and Aunt Betty were both dead.

I was proud to know such a gifted man. He also professionally illustrated the 'Boy's Own' magazines. He was a brilliant artist and all I wanted, when he died, was one of his pictures and a 'Boy's Own'. Unfortunately, when Aunt Betty died, Dorothy married and became a Jehovah's Witness, so all Uncle's worldly goods were sold, including his art – I was terribly saddened by this.

In those days there were only three 'recognised' levels of Christian Worship, any others weren't talked about much. If you were a Weslyan, like my Aunt Alice who was posh, you were 'top of the scale'; if you were Congregationalist you came next, but if you were 'Primitive' you were 'the bottom set'. It was 'Weslies', 'Congs' and 'Prims' in that order.

During the Second World War a bomb dropped directly onto the Wesleyan Chapel, demolishing it. I don't know where they went then; C of E or Catholics perhaps?

The Salvation Army was hardly known of then, but they made their mark wherever help was needed and pretty soon it was known that 'The bonnets can get in anywhere', before even a parson's collar.

CHAPTER 26

Returning Home

Joan at nineteen.

When the war was over I was nineteen and Mam and Dad wanted me home again. I found out that they had been paying for me to stay in Glaisdale, though I was never told how much of course. I never really knew how Mam and Dad saw me, as a person, it will always be a mystery to me.

Aunt and Uncle cried when I had to leave, especially Uncle; Aunt didn't show her feelings easily. I never knew if she and Uncle were in love or not. They shared the same double bed but Uncle always wore his shirt and long-combs, with his cap and trousers nearby, "In case of air-raids."

"The on'y time awd Hitler wad come on t'moors, wad be for a sheep for his dinner!" an old Yorkshire woman once said. Whitby was shelled in the First War. It had some bombing in the last war too, like Scarborough, but not severe.

Anyway here I was, having to pack my things and close up the summer house. Uncle Robert and Aunt Winnie came to fetch me, with the motor bike and side-car, and there was continued crying. I don't like to think about that; I was so sad to be saying goodbye to a life I'd never experience again. There had been some dark times but soon forgotten, and not worth thinking about. I would always miss the moors and woods of Glaisdale.

Arriving home was a bit strange but I surprised myself at how easily I slipped back into the old ways, picking up with my friends and joining the youth club in town. Aunt Winnie had a Pekinese I got to know a bit. Wong was a funny little chap and very faithful, but whenever he was offered a treat he would sniff and sniff looking really worried, as if he thought he was going to be poisoned. He didn't trust anything unless it was in his dish.

I had a lot of catching up to do and my life changed for the better. No more pills or hospitals, or living a quiet life. I was back on the 'band wagon' again. It was good to have time with Mam and we would go brambling together, or just for walks sometimes.

The nicest walk I had with her was away up Loy Lane, past the many allotments, where she had her own allotment and where the local chaps, many retired, spent most of their days. They each had their little sheds, done out with a bit of carpet, maybe an oil-stove, a chair and a thermos of tea, besides their tools and seedlings. Other chaps would crowd in each other's little huts and chatter away, smoking their 'Woodbines', going home only for a bit of supper – fish and chips and a listen to the radio, then bed.

An easy, laid-back life and very contented. We never needed much in those days. A good walk was as good as a tonic.

This particular day Mam and I arrived at the first gate which let us through to the first field, then we walked around by an overgrown ditch until the far field with one old house; home to three families during my lifetime.

There was no laid-on water, gas or electricity, but they made out a life for themselves regardless. Mam and I might stop and gossip, then carry on through a tiny gate into Bramble Lane, thickly overgrown and leading to a plantation where we wandered through thickly padded paths of pine-needles, breathing in that wonderful smell only a pine plantation has.

Suddenly a shaft of brilliant sunlight shot down between the trees, seemingly preventing us from crossing. We stood for a few minutes, staring into the beam; seeing a multitude of living things, things which share with us every day of our lives, in thousands of specks of dust.

I imagined many fairy things at that moment. Mam said, "A beam from God, how wonderful."

Mam had spent years at Sunday School, teaching and

playing the organ, and once, when missionaries came, was asked to join them in their travels. Granny would not let her go; she was only sixteen at the time. I wonder what her life would have been…

The beam of sunlight faded and we turned back to take another path to the open road, but it was then that my idea for a fairy tale gathered itself into my mind. Over recent years I finally got that fairy tale completed but as yet never published.

Mam and I finished our walk, going down towards High Town, another little hamlet, which brought us home again to East Loftus where we had a good tea of Mam's home-made bread and jam and her gorgeous cheesecakes.

Mam still had her allotment and was busy weeding one Sunday, down at the bottom near the stream, when she looked up and saw Aunty Winnie coming down the path carrying a cardboard box. She had been crying. Uncle Rob followed carrying a spade.

"What's wrong Winnie?" Mam had asked. "What's going on?"

"Wong's died," wept Aunt Winnie, "we've come to bury him, can you give us a space?"

"Well aye, anywhere ah won't be digging – ah won't want to dig 'im up."

"Well," she told me afterwards, "that was a procession that was."

So Wong lies up yonder in Loy Lane. They both never expected to have another dog, but Charley arrived, a pretty Cavalier, He outlived both Uncle Rob and Aunt Winnie. Kate, their Granddaughter, took him but he didn't live long after.

I never forgot Aunt Betty and Uncle Walter, writing and visiting often, sometimes taking my friends with me. They were both ageing a bit now.

Mam, Dad and I just went on from where we left off and it was good to discover one of my old pals, Evelyn, had taken to visiting Mam. She had lost her own mother and she and Mam became almost like mother and daughter over the years.

CHAPTER 27

The Lost Teeth

I was surprised to discover Mam's teeth came out, and would watch fascinated as she brushed her sets, top and bottom, then just stuffed them back in her mouth. How was it she never swallowed them, I wondered?

I was worried on the occasion when Aunt Betty lost her teeth.

One day a friend brought a fresh crab, which were scarce. We had a good feast but, come night-time, Aunt was sick, very much so, having to get out of bed three or four times and rush to the bathroom.

At about four o'clock in the morning I heard her cry out, "Walter! My top set has gone down the pan and I've pulled the chain! Oh what will I do without them?" she wailed. "I'll look awful!" and she wept.

"Oh, all right Betty, we'll look for them. I'll get Joan up and then dig up the manhole, we might be lucky. If you're sick again don't pull the chain." He knocked on my door. "Away, get up, Auntie's teeth have gone down t'pan – we're going to look for 'em!"

We trudged down the stairs and out into the garden. It was still dark and we daren't shine a torch, because it was wartime, so with matches we found the metal drain cover after digging up the lawn. It was cold and damp and I was shivering as we got the lid cleared, around five in the morning, and were about to lift it up when the postman came by.

"Way noo then, Walter, what's thee deein' at this tahm of a mornin' – buryin' t'missus?" he cackled. It must have been a bit surprising for him to see us both digging like that, and Uncle did tell him what had happened, but must have wished he hadn't. Billy 'Postie' went off still cackling – it would be all around the village in no time.

Finally the lid was up, Uncle shone the torch in. "Now, see if you can see him near t'bend." I looked and there was Auntie's top set. "By gaw, that's a bit of luck!" exclaimed Uncle, stretching down and retrieving the teeth.

Aunt put the teeth in disinfectant for about a week. She certainly was pleased to have them back.

Uncle kept his teeth on a saucer behind a candlestick on the mantelpiece and I had to carry them up to him – ugh!

I seem to have had rather too many contacts with other folk's false teeth; there were my husband's fangs, later on in my life – two teeth on a small wire, and he didn't always remember to put them in. After about a year they were left in a jam jar for decades, grinning at me. Eventually Victor threw them out.

Then there was his pal, Meredith, who had one fang. He bit into an apple, ate it and threw the core into the fire before he realised his fang was missing. "My fang has gone!" They tried to retrieve it but it fell through the grate still hanging on to the apple core. Next morning his wife found the black, sizzled core with a melted fang still clinging to it. Thank goodness I've never had to have false teeth!

CHAPTER 28

Shopping With Mam

Evelyn and I would go shopping with Mam some days, though Evelyn would say, "Eee, what she be like today?" Dad gave up going with her, he'd be so embarrassed. Mam was known very well by the local shopkeepers.

I think we felt sorry for Mr Gaston. He had the little shop where all my sensible shoes came from – lace-up brogues. Mr Gaston must have been a very patient man

We would all go into his shop and Mam would ask him for a pair of 'sensible shoes in good quality'.

"Right, Mrs Dickens, let's see what we've got; any particular colour and what size?"

"Ah, size five and Ah think brown, or perhaps a nice cream."

Down would come the boxes and opened up, then a long succession of trying on shoe after shoe. "Well," Mam would say, "some are a bit tight," or, "one is a bit loose, and ahm not sure about the cream; a bit light in colour – ah don't know really, can ah think about it and come in again?" Evelyn and I were mortified. He'd smile, poor man, pack up the boxes and replace them. I wonder what he said under his breath as she'd remark, "Well ahm not buying what ah don't like, so there!" to all the customers who'd be waiting their turn.

I think the worst shopping day was in Whitby. We had

gone to look for a new teapot; an earthenware type. We went into 'Tinner Halls', a nickname for the local ironmonger, in Golden Lion Bank.

"Ah'd like a new teapot, one in brown pottery with a good spout."

Out came various teapots. Mam examined the lids and handles, peered inside, put them down, picked them up again and fiddled about. "How much are they?"

He told her.

"Oh, a little bit more than ah wanted to pay," said Mam, "er, ah like this one, could you just put a drop of water in, if you don't mind, and ah'll try pouring it out on t'step."

The man looked boggle-eyed. He did actually pour some water in, quite miffed. Mam walked to the shop door, pulled it open and poured the water out all over the step. Evelyn and I would have hidden away if we could.

"Quite satisfactory," said Mam, and she took out her purse to pay him.

He wrapped it up for her. "Thank you madam." He still looked a bit boggle-eyed though, as we all walked out of the shop.

That wasn't the end of her shopping spree. Over the bridge we went into the old market area where there was a broom shop. Every kind of broom and brush, from paint brushes and scrubbing brushes to nail brushes and shoe brushes were there.

"Ah want a hearth brush, to sweep around t'grate where cinders fall out," Mam announced.

"I'm not coming in," Evelyn whispered, and she stood outside.

Mam asked a young man for a "Smallish hearth brush, just for sweeping around t'tiles you see?"

"Yes madam." He brought two or three nice little hand brushes out from the back room.

Mam felt the bristles, she then pushed some things on the counter away to one side and brushed the counter down. The young man looked aghast but Mam bought the brush. "A nice little man, that," Mam said as we went for the bus.

"What did she do?" Evelyn asked.

"Oh, just brushed the counter." I laughed.

We both gave up going into Sayers the grocer shop, in Loftus, with her. In fact the shop girls would push one another when they saw her coming. "It's Mrs Dickens, ahm not servin' 'er – 'ere you go out Mavis, don't ask me!"

"An' don't ask me neither!" another would say. In the end the boss had to do it.

"Well, ah want what ah want when ah go into a shop," Mam would say. "There's no point if they can't find what you want." I can hear her saying it to this day. She'd even open up sealed goods. "Ah want to see 'em properly, they might be dried up or smell queer."

The local butcher frightened her and she had come home in a state. "Old Gibson banged his knife on t'counter in front of me. He's upset me!"

"What, did he threaten you?" I cried, ready to go down and tell him off. I didn't really want to.

Mam told me, "As ah always do, ah asked him for a nice little neat piece of lean meat, no fat or blood, an' wiped nice an' dry. He cut me two joints, not what ah wanted, an' then clattered his knife down with a bang. Ah thought he'd gone crazy – ah won't go in there again! Ah'll find somewhere else that will serve me."

I went down, and she came with me, but the shop was shut. We knocked on the house door but nobody answered. I told Mam to forget it; she needn't go there again anyway, and we went home. She thought he might have killed her but I bet old Gibson was glad she never went in any more.

When she was in the Saltburn Nursing Home the owner had a man come in every now and then, bringing in underwear and dresses etc. for the old folk. Mam went to look at the clothing and we tried to persuade her to buy two simple frocks for £6.50 each.

"Ahm not payin' all that! Scandalous!"

The owner, Diane, said, "Tell her they're only five shillings and eleven pence."

I did and Mam bought them.

Poor old Mam. I daren't behave as she did in shops. As she got much older, Dad, in his retirement, did the shopping. She never got used to the 'new money'. She couldn't understand there were no more shilling notes, two shillings now being a ten pence coin. As for a pound being a coin and not a note, or a shilling being five 'p', let alone the other decimal coins, she was simply puzzled by them.

There was really no place for poor old Mam in this fast and modern world. She was ninety-eight when she died.

CHAPTER 29

The Drawing Office

I was twenty before I was fully employed, back at home. Dad found me a job as a tracer in the drawing offices. He was a senior accountant at Skinningrove Iron and Steel Works, situated across the cliffs, with a long jetty running out into the sea, about four miles away; the furnaces pounding and thumping all day, and when they were 'turned out', at night, the sky became scarlet.

One got used to the sounds; they meant, as long as they sounded, men had the security of work. It was the mainstay for the large area around, being built in a most wonderful part of the North East.

When I went for my interview there, Dad said to be sure I was smartly dressed, so I wore a suit and even a hat. The Chief of Draughtsmen was an elderly, old fashioned man; German, and highly intelligent. He asked the usual questions, took an interest in the fact that I gathered wild flowers, and was actually thrilled that I planted a peanut in a pot at the office. '*Arachis hypogaea*' he called it, and I saw how eccentric he seemed to be, but quite a gentleman for all that.

I got the job.

At the time he had just lost one of his sons in an accident. I don't recall exactly what happened but it was a shocking time for him.

I took over the youth club canteen and joined their drama group, growing in confidence all the time. Now and again my old condition played me up, but then I would take off with my paints, on a bus to Runswick Bay, and sit on the lovely cliffs painting, then go down onto the splendid beach to gather pebbles and shells, for the little models I had taken to making.

Every August some of us would have days out at Whitby, going by steam train; sixpence down to Skinningrove or maybe one shilling on to Whitby. What a clean beach stretching out along to Sands End. These were the sands so admired by Lewis Carroll, who wrote *The Walrus and the Carpenter* with this very stretch in mind – my favourite of his verses.

Granny would organise the day out, with Mam and me, our Dennis, Aunt Winnie and Uncle Rob, Great Aunt Edie and Great Uncle Alf, and sometimes Great Aunt Jane who was, as Aunt Winnie said, "As deaf as a post."

"Hey," Uncle Rob would say, "awd Jane laughing agean – she doesn't know what about, she's nivver 'eard us talkin'."

Aunt Winnie looked after Great Aunt Jane and, in the war time, slept over with her in the big feather bed when Alf and Edie were away in Durham. "Aye, she's 'ad me awake 'alf the night, wakenin' me up three or fower tahms, pokin' me, 'Let me out our Winnie, Ah need 'po.' Why she insists to sleepin' agen t'wall ah don't know, she won't sleep on t'edge side. Ah's sick on it!"

"Wey, don't keep goin' down then," Uncle Rob would say, "stop at 'ome."

Poor Aunt Jane, I really loved her. She never married and I don't know if she ever had a young man, I only remember she did fall in love with a singer from Loftus who travelled with a famous singer, Richard Tauber of many years ago. I can't remember the local boy's name. How sad to love someone who would never know; who probably never even noticed you other than just as a friend.

Skinningrove. Where Kilton Beck finds its way to the sea we come to the Ironstone Mining District of Skinningrove, Loftus and Brotton. The drifts, or 'winnings', were driven into the earth and the Ironworks perched on top of the cliff in a cloud of red dust and sulphur. Skinningrove lies along the steep sides of a ravine. Row upon row of identical small, terraced, miner's cottages run down to the shore, all clean and neat and unique in this industrial setting. Skinningrove is no holiday resort but it possesses rare quality not found elsewhere. Beauty is in the eye of the beholder!

Bridges at Skinningrove. The old bridge at the bottom is the bridge to Beck Row. Above it new bridge, built in 1920, carried traffic which formerly had to drive through the water, u Skinningrove Bank and Hummersea Lane.

After three years I still wasn't good at my tracing; it was very tedious work, and I couldn't print as well as the other girls. Looking out of the office windows I watched the local kids, and dogs from the village, running along the beach and in and out of the sea. I spent my lunch breaks joining them in the fine weather.

It was an interesting stretch of beach with loads of rocks and fossils everywhere, and amazing shore plants. I felt free as air while rushing around, with the dogs especially, who would charge about in a body chasing the driftwood or seaweed I threw around and bringing them back. It was great fun.

Folks just let their dogs out of the tiny, drab little 'two-up, two-down' dwellings. They were rough folk, and hard workers.

I recalled Mam telling me, when she was a girl and Granny and Granddad lived for a time in one of those houses, she said how poor the kids were, Granddad being a miner. If she was eating an apple the kids would crowd around her and beg for the apple core she left, and they begged a bite of her sandwiches at lunch time. Mam was one of the lucky ones.

As far as I know the village is still poor to this day...

I knew I had to get out of the office and go back to work in the open somewhere. I didn't get on with the draughtsmen nor they with me, apart from one Polish guy – I think I missed my chance with him. He was good looking and we were good friends. He came to our house a lot; Mam liked him a lot too... I often wondered what became of him; did he marry? I never saw him again after he left the works.

Office work really wasn't for me; it affected my eyes and I had to wear glasses in the end. Dad was disappointed when I gave in my notice, of course, but I think I would have got the sack anyway, if I hadn't left of my own accord. For a few weeks I hung around doing nothing in particular, just messing about painting and getting nowhere.

CHAPTER 30

Going Off To Scotland

"So, what are you going to do, now you've left your job?" Mam wanted to know.

Dad didn't say much.

"Advertise," I said.

"What about?"

"Well, poultry farming; I'd love to be a proper poultry maid."

"So where do you think you'll go then?"

"More or less anywhere." And so the conversation went on.

I had had my twenty-second birthday when I advertised in *The Lady*, a lesser-known magazine, and perhaps not read amongst farming folk so much, so I only had three replies.

One was a young chap who sent me a photograph of him holding a saxophone, and a letter telling me about himself and wishing to meet me. I think he wanted a woman, not a poultry maid, so that was a no, no.

The second was from a retired military man in Cornwall, offering me the job of poultry maid, also telling me I would live in a caravan and must be of good appearance. Cheek of him – no, no, no.

The third was from an educated person, requiring an extra poultry maid on his farm with 13,000 head of poultry;

'Thomas Blackburn & Son Ltd. 'The Dinning', Closeburne, Dumfries.' This sounded magnificent. I applied, arranged to meet, travelling up to Dumfries by coach, was met at the coach station and taken to a hotel where I would stay overnight.

I had never stayed in a hotel alone and was nervous. I was shown my room and given times for breakfast, then I left my overnight bag and went for my interview, still nervous.

An elegant woman interviewed me. She was Mrs Blackburn. She said she was impressed by my letter and introduced me to her young son, who offered his hand to shake mine. He was three years old. I shook hands as if he was an adult.

That got me the job. Actions speak louder than words!

Mam wasn't too happy I was leaving England!

I shared a bedroom with a little dumpy girl who had a hare lip. She recited Burns to me at night, in a lispy voice. She wasn't very clean or hygienic. Her father was a well-known chemist and her mother wrote children's books. Their name was Lockie. She only stayed for three months more after I arrived.

The wardens of the hostels were true Scots. The wife, getting on a bit, was the prettiest old lady I'd ever met; full of life and fun. She was so entertaining and her husband, a rather dour Scotsman, told us all his life story, including the fact that his ancestor was Robert the Bruce.

Robbie Burns' brother had worked on this same old farmland, but as a cattle man. He was Gilbert Burns and had slept in the hostel's little loft room.

I had a great time in Dumfries. The boss was a gentleman; his manager, a Welshman was quite the opposite, he was one of the rudest men I ever met, with a wife not much better; she would, disgustingly, call out, "I'll muck on you!" if we slightly upset her, horrible woman. I soon fell out with them.

After six months of working with so many chickens, learning so much, and trekking down by the Nith riverside, discovering many rare wild flowers, I felt free and, apart from the Welshman, quite happy. I sang 'La Bella Marguerita' to the 500 pullets I was in charge of, instead of 'chuck, chuck'. They all came running, flapping, scuttling and squawking, squashing down a large patch of wild thyme growing in the field. I remember the smell of crushed thyme with great affection.

In one of the larger laying sheds I fell over a stone, embedded in the earthen floor. I scrambled up and pulled at the stone in annoyance; if I'd been carrying a bucket of eggs they would have been scrambled eggs.

As I removed the stone I discovered a nest of fleas and in seconds they were all over my body. I dropped the stone and ran back into the hostel where I ran myself a bath, throwing in my clothes as well. Footsteps came running along the landing and a fist hammered on the door, "Who's in there!?" It was Mrs Ferguson. "My brother has been waiting for the water heating up for his bath!"

"Sorry Mrs Ferguson, my clothes are covered in fleas and they're all on my body, it's the only thing I could think of doing, I would have infested the hostel otherwise."

Joan and hens.

"Fleas! Fleas! What fleas? It's a poultry farm."

"No, this is an infestation, I'll leave the water for you to see."

"My brother is very annoyed."

"Well, I am sorry."

Mrs Ferguson hurried off to explain to her brother and I had to wash my clothes as best I could.

I loved all the poultry of course, working with laying hens and carrying large metal buckets full of eggs; what a weight to carry.

Speaking of carrying, there was water, hay, straw, and even the need to move huts in order to spray them with creosote. It got in our eyes and on our skin and, by gum, it stung!

We – three other girls and one boy – bagged up corn and trolleyed it around, but it was harder than I ever imagined. I found it too hard in the end. The manager didn't think I was strong enough and I was asked to leave; he even tried to be nice but I was heartbroken and left in tears.

Years later my husband, Victor, myself and our daughter Belinda, went to visit 'The Dinning'. I was 40 and saddened to see the hostel, still there, had been turned into a private house; the huts, sheds, and breeding pens all gone and the fields silent. It was strange that so much life had ceased, with

Thomas Blackburn and his son now retired it was the end of another chapter.

I remember the journey home. There was a farm manager, from the adjoining piggery, whose wife used to invite me over to them on days off. We saw them again and this plump, rosy-faced wife with their little son, promised to wave white cloths as the train passed. I watched, and they did – I just cried.

The Dinning Poultry Farm:
Basil, Tessa, Gilbert, Mr and Mrs Fergusson.

Gilbert, Maisie, Fiona Locke and Fruchan in Mrs Fergusson's arms.

CHAPTER 31

The Mistake

When I came back from Scotland I stayed home for about seven weeks, hoping I'd find a job somewhere again. Mam had contemplated buying a place with a bit of land, so I could try my hand at a bit of poultry keeping, but it wasn't to be.

We went to see a place in Sands End, a fine-looking house up the road from the beach, with some land at the back. It bore the name 'Thalassa' and we were shown around the premises, but Mam didn't like the atmosphere. I think she had a sense of foreboding, and a neighbour later told us, there, about the young man who had been selling up to move to a better job.

I'm not sure if he was a pilot or not, but he had, unfortunately, just lost his life in a plane. It's so long ago I can't remember details clearly, but obviously he would not be the one selling the house now and Mam refused to consider it.

Nothing else turned up for me. Her strange feelings always got in the way, so I decided I would go down to Watford, where my two close friends had moved to. They were the Dudleys, and their little girl Paula. I had felt terribly bereft when they moved away from Yorkshire, where we had spent a lot of time together and had a good friendship.

I was invited to go and stay with them, so booked the long train journey and set off. On arriving in Kings Cross, Jim Dudley met me and we were soon in a tube train. What a terrifying experience. I have never liked the tubes and try to avoid them whenever I can.

How my life was to change.

Dot and little Paula made me most welcome. I had a happy holiday and enjoyed myself so much I just got the feeling I'd like to stay down south, so I wrote home and told Mam and Dad I would be staying on. No doubt they would be upset.

However I was with the Dudleys for over six months and found a job there, for the time being, back in an office as a tracer for bottle washing machines, because I was desperate.

It didn't work. I was given the sack. I was not a tracer.

However I had become friends with the head tracer, who ran a rambling group which I joined. There I found a girl called Joan, who was employed as a poultry maid and, believe it or not, she told me she was leaving to go home and look after her mother, who was ill.

After we had chatted she asked if I would be interested in taking her place. She was employed by a retired Colonel in Chorley Wood, a beautiful village in Buckingham.

I got the job and it was great; a smallholding and gardens. The Colonel was elderly, his wife years younger and rather snobby. I had a most beautiful room at the top of a chalet bungalow. There were two children, Penelope who was attending ballet school at the age of ten, and Anthony who was an excitable kiddy and often mischievous, for instance turning on the water pump and filling my egg-basket.

Anyway I was soon busily employed. It was great to be back in the open air with chickens and turkeys. There were also three Chinese Runner ducks and some big geese.

I got quite friendly with the geese; they were as good as guard dogs, honking loudly whenever a stranger approached. The old gander, Sen, did not like men – he soon made that clear by chasing after them, grabbing their turn ups and not letting go; he was seemingly a 'ladies' man'...!

There was one other man employed there, Hans, a Dutchman in his late thirties. I loved his broken English, especially when he informed me, every Thursday that, "The jenlmens who empty da dustbins are 'ere." I was amused by his 'jenlmens'.

I had various adventures here, not least the evening forty-eight turkeys disappeared. I had been feeding them up for Christmas and on this occasion I went to shut them in for the night only to find the shed empty. I had several horrified thoughts running through my mind, as I went to report the disappearance to the Colonel, not least the worry of badgers or foxes getting them.

We took large torches and shone all around searching. There was a large patch of stinging nettles a little way away and I noticed little pinpoints of something shining. I went nearer and heard a faint 'gobble, gobble' – their eyes had given them away and I called the Colonel over.

There, huddled together, were the foolish birds; they had decided to 'sleep out'. The stars were shining, but there was no moon and we had to flush them out with great difficulty, hardly able to keep track of the whole flock with just our torches. What a performance! We finally got them all into the turkey house and were relieved next morning to find we hadn't missed any – all forty-eight were there thank goodness.

There was an orchard there as well, and next door a field full of cattle. It was autumn and there were a lot of windfalls. The Colonel hadn't noticed that part of his fence was down. It wasn't long before we had an irate farmer coming round complaining his cows were drunk. Of course they had been feasting on the fallen apples which had begun fermenting in their stomachs, and there they were, stumbling around merrily – I hope it didn't curdle their milk...

Something more serious happened on another occasion, when I went to let the young pullets out one morning. I found the boards which fastened each end of the slatted coops had been pulled away. Chickens were lying about half eaten; some inside were still alive but with damaged legs; they had been snapped off through the slats. I was appalled at the carnage. Of course the poor injured birds had to be destroyed.

The Colonel was convinced it was the work of a badger and spent nights waiting with his gun, hoping to catch the intruders to no avail.

CHAPTER 32

Courting

Before I actually began this new job, I was on one of the rambles and we were about two miles down the road from Kings Langley railway station. We had left details there, of our trek, for any latecomers. I was at the back of the group and I turned round. Coming up behind us was a very big chap, black hair, dark glasses and over six feet tall, with a moustache, and wearing a leather jacket that squeaked as he walked.

When he caught up with us he had a word with Margery, our leader. It seems he was supposed to be with 'The Holiday Fellowship' from North London, who had also left details, at the same station, of their route. When he had asked at the ticket office they had mistakenly given him our details.

Margery welcomed him, "Why not join us for the day?" and he fell in alongside me. Who was he? One Victor Scher, from London, owning his own small dry cleaning business and flat, aged 30 and single, that is until he met me.

We went out for eleven months before we married. We were not romantic; people weren't, as a rule, up north, so we were very down to earth, though we did have our moments!

Victor often bought me buttered Brazils or a bunch of old-fashioned Calendula, generally known as Marigolds. Sometimes he ate most of the sweets himself, especially if he was delayed, and would be popping them into his mouth while he waited. I would be presented with the few he had left... he never fancied boxes of expensive chocolates and my engagement ring was second hand, with a small sapphire and two diamond chippings – the wedding ring was £10 – he was careful...

Victor, 1949.   *Henry, 1945.*

Victor Scher.

I lost them both after about ten years, somewhere in our garden, which was concreted over to park Victor's furniture van, motorbike and side-car and a smaller van, so no-one will ever find my rings. I was upset I'd lost them. He bought me a new wedding ring, but not an engagement ring. (I always hoped to have another engagement ring, and I did get one when I celebrated my 80th birthday – one with a sapphire, costing £100.)

We often 'went Dutch' when we were out somewhere. There was the occasional kiss and once, when we were visiting Loftus, I was sitting on Victor's knee and the remark came back, "He nivver left her alone five minutes!" We never canoodled in front of Mam – she was terrified because he was so big she thought he would squash me…!

Victor was very practical and an excellent cook (which was just as well because I hate cooking). His mother taught him – she was a wonderful cook.

He proposed to me in Chorley Wood, whilst sitting amongst the bluebells, and a cuckoo actually called 'cuckoo' sat in a nearby tree. I remarked, "Here we are, three cuckoos together!" Fate had us meet 'by mistake' and we were together for fifty-four years, man and wife. How's that...?

Our wedding was different. Victor was a Jewish boy; his family were Liberal Jews and welcomed me. I was very fortunate they were so broad-minded. They were good people; all accepted the fact that I was a 'Shiska' – I'm not sure if I have that right, but it is a Hebrew slang term for non-Jews, not that Victor ever used the Yiddish.

I did not wish to be married up in Yorkshire. Why? My friends and neighbours thought it amusing that Victor was such a massive man, unusual for a Jewish male, and referred to us as 'Little and Large'. I was hurt at their rudeness. They never thought I would ever 'get a fellow' but, not only were they wrong, I 'got' one twice as big as anybody else's.

Going ahead with our plans, we decided to be married in Willesden Green Registry Office, to save Mam and Dad, and only immediate family, the embarrassment of such ridicule. Victor wore his dark overcoat, with a red carnation in the lapel, and I wore a mulberry red suit. Victor's parents, Mummy and Daddy Scher I called them, made arrangements for the wedding breakfast to be held at Willsden Green, in their quite large flat.

The Dudleys were upset that their little girl was not to be a bridesmaid after all, but they had a special invitation, after the honeymoon, to 'Mummy's' lovely evening meal. It didn't help Paula stop being upset and I did feel mean. I realised I shouldn't have promised her anything. How often do we make such rash promises?

I always said they would never play the Wedding March for me. I didn't know why I said it at the time I said it but, sure enough, there was no way it could be played at the Civic Office ceremony.

There were just fourteen of us in the end, including Victor's brother and wife, sister, the parents and two other ladies. Miss Eglington, the governess from the small poultry farm in Chorley Wood making thirteen. 'Mummy' Scher was superstitious, so she invited her cleaning woman to make fourteen. I liked Eggy, as the Colonel's children had nicknamed the governess, we got on well together and she was quite honoured to be invited.

After the ceremony at the Registry Office, we were driven back to Mummy and Daddy's flat and, as I walked in up the stairs, Mummy switched on their ancient gramophone. Someone had found a gramophone record of the Wedding March for her and she played it for me as I entered.

Daddy Scher.

Mam and Dad seemed to enjoy the wedding; the meal was amazing. I don't think they could have coped with it up north, with Jewish guests and a whole churchful of relatives and friends who would have expected to come, not to mention the local folk crowding to gape and no doubt gossip. Not likely. The local folk weren't very pleased; I had 'diddled' them – I had but it was my day, so there.

I hadn't been married above a twelve month when I met little Mrs Snowdon from East Loftus. She had nine kids, reasonably well behaved, on pain of Dad undoing his trouser belt – then they'd get it.

"Aye," said Mrs Snowdon, "a bit of advice if tha's goin' to have babbies – if any one on 'em starts a carry on give 'em a good 'idin' and then when they're yellin' give 'em another yan to mek 'em shurrup." And she went off cackling.

CHAPTER 33

Bad Things

When we were in our thirties, Victor and I decided to adopt a child and mentioned our intentions to our local GP. His reply was fascinating; he had been a ship's surgeon and now had his own practise, and we'd been with him for nine years.

He could see how upset we were, still having no children, and said he'd look into it. When he called us out of the blue one day we were pleased to hear there might be a baby we could adopt. We weren't so happy about the circumstances though.

One of his social friends had 'got into trouble', her partner had been gone a few years leaving one child, then she'd married again, an epileptic. Stella had applied to be his housekeeper – six months later he asked her to marry him, which she did, but his health failed and finally he died. Stella was then pregnant.

Doctor Fisher explained that this child was illegitimate, and Stella was thinking of putting the baby into an orphanage because she had no home, no job and no Social Services to help her. It was the 50s; such aid wasn't available then, unlike the help single mothers have today. Annie, her other child, was eleven and it was hard for her too. He simply asked, "Are you interested?"

We certainly were. We arranged a visit to the Buckinghamshire village where Stella lived, and met her and the loveliest baby we had ever seen. We were delighted, and within months we had our own little one. Poor Stella was devastated. She'd named the baby Claire, but we renamed her Belinda when she was ours at last. What a wonderful life we had ahead, with such a beautiful baby.

When Stella visited for the last time I watched as she left, and saw her break down as she went. She didn't know I was watching and I don't know how she ever reached her way back to Saint Peter's Village, where she was staying.

Belinda was, and is, the greatest miracle in our lives. Victor 'worshipped the ground she walked on' as the saying goes, and life was amazing for us. There were always people in and out, lots of children too, and we joined a Pentecostal Church which gave us a Faith at last.

Belinda, 6 month, with Toffee and her pup Bunty.

CHAPTER 34

The Bungalow

Victor and I went to see it. A very promising semi-detached, with a large garden shed and chicken huts at the far end of a two hundred foot piece of land. Oh yes, we bought it.

The owner who showed us around was a bit eccentric. The 'hen huts' had been kennels for Alsatians; she kept about five of them. The one she had with her, at the time we were looking over the property, had been ordered into a corner and a chair placed in front of him. He eyed us and I was somewhat worried.

The owner said she was finding a home for him, would we take him? I said, "Sorry, no." We already had our dog and cat, and I couldn't have trusted this dog. I hope he did find a good home though; he was too big for me.

We moved in, in good weather, but Toffee kept leaping out of the bungalow windows and running off. This was a problem. I was grateful to a couple of local kids, Sandra and Alex with a dog named Jaguar, who visited us often, because they used to find Toffee and bring her home again, for which I rewarded them. These two were 'latchkey kids'. Their mother and father worked all day but I loved having them both.

Cinders settled in very well; she was a dear little cat.

We found most neighbours friendly, except the one on our right, who was a miserable type and ended up causing us problems. There was also a 'little something' about the bungalow itself, which didn't diminish our happiness in having a proper house at last; it was just a feeling.

These were happy times, especially when our Church friends came back for coffee and snacks in the evenings. Pastor and Mrs Price were now our Spiritual Parents, but was there 'something' in the bungalow which didn't like our new life and true friends?

Victor, by this time, was doing curtain fitting, stocking repairs with several women working for him, had a new man doing most of the upholstery repairs, and was still dry cleaning.

11, Nicholl's Avenue. With Toffe's pups and Sandra Kirk, and Wendy Ekin, Belinda's Godmother.

He always yearned for shop premises. Little did we know what was going to turn up in later years. He bought me cockerels to fatten up for Christmas, to sell amongst the neighbours, plus a few laying hens. The hens were a success but the cockerels kept fighting, and would do so to the death – blood everywhere – so no more cockerels…

I grew all kinds of plants and flowers, etc. Everything seemed hunky dory, though there was no sign of a family and we felt out of it with no children.

Toffee was still running away and one day came back in a flurry. It was a week or two before we realised she was 'in pup' – now what were we going to do? The day we thought she was going to give birth she seemed to be having trouble.

We took her to a vet up in town, who said I had left her too long, and he induced the pups. There were six of them, and Toffee brought them up well enough but she would keep getting out and running away so, sadly, she had to go, once they were old enough, because she could have caused accidents. We missed her though.

We kept one of the puppies, a little black and brown female with whitish patches, short legs and a lovely fluffy tail. I had to pull her out because she stuck as she was being born, poor Toffee. We called the puppy Bunty. She looked like a Welsh Corgi with long fur. We had her for sixteen years.

CHAPTER 35

The Move

Belinda always knew she had two mummies; one where she came from her tummy and loved her very much, and me, her second mummy who adored her. She was six years old when Victor found the shop with the upstairs flat. It had a kitchen at the back of the shop and a long garden with sheds. Victor liked it and bought it – we were on the move again!

Before this Belinda and I had gone to Chipperfield, to stay with Christian friends for a few months because I was unwell, so Victor had to manage alone, until we moved into the new shop premises. While we were away he took in three Chinese lodgers.

I wasn't sure what to make of that. I'd gone with Belinda and the dog and he'd replaced us with three Chinese men...

Belinda did love it with Aunty Monica and Uncle Cyril. She went to school in Watford, where Uncle Cyril was a teacher, with their older son, John.

Monica ran a private nursery school and I helped her and Aunty Daisy, who lived in a separate part of the house with Cyril's mam.

Victor would visit from time to time and was doing well. The shop was still to be ours when I was well enough to return.

I did enjoy those months. Monica and I, both being dyslexic, would make so many silly blunders but we would collapse with laughter. I really began to feel better.

I had been in hospital with nervous problems for a few weeks and eventually told them I couldn't stay there any longer; I didn't feel mentally ill, just suffering shock. We spent ten days in Yorkshire with Mam and Dad then Victor came to fetch us in our Grand Humber Snipe, a large saloon car from the 1920s. As we were travelling back we went out of control, skidded across a dual carriageway and crashed into an upright fence, past a field full of sheep. Victor had dozed off, it seems.

Bunty, our little dog, suitcases and I were jammed into the backs of the front seats; Belinda had been 'shot' under the dashboard and the steering wheel had thumped into Victor's chest. We were dazed but not seriously injured; more shocked than anything. It was amazing we escaped so lightly.

A farmer, driving his tractor, came across to where we had crashed. No concern for our welfare, he just started straight in about us having to exchange addresses and we'd have to pay for the damaged fence; he'd send us the bill. He didn't even ask after Belinda, who was crying with the shock. It beggars belief. Of course we wanted to pay for the damage – that should have gone without saying. He sent us the bill all right, miserable so and so.

We had a very shaky journey home, badly bruised. I was particularly shaken because it brought back to me the time I was under that car as a child.

We kept in touch with Monica and Cyril for forty years, and they came to visit us. Even after we'd returned north, in the 50s, they still came to see us.

Victor's new shop had been a pet shop and he asked me if I'd like half the premises to keep it the same. I jumped at the chance and it worked out quite well. Belinda, of course, was delighted, so I now had a pet shop. Victor was to clear up the last of the stuff in the bungalow; his desk and papers were still there and needed sorting, but he would then pack the van with the last of our stuff and lock the place up. Suddenly the telephone rang and Belinda answered it. "It's Dad," she said, and then went off to her new bedroom.

Victor was breathless. "Are you both all right?" he gasped.

"Why, yes."

"I'll be home in a few minutes."

"What's wrong?"

"I'm out of here now; I'll tell you when I get there." He banged the phone down.

I was startled; what was going on?

I heard him bang the van door and he rushed upstairs, "Where's Belinda?"

"She's in bed, tell me what happened?"

"I was clearing up my papers and packing them into the boxes when I heard Belinda coughing. I ran to the nursery but of course Belinda wasn't there. I was scared but rushed back to finish packing. I still hadn't put the alarm clock in; it was on top of the desk and – it was *pushed* off. It didn't topple, I saw it and it fell onto a pile of papers on the desk flap with a thump.

"I struggled to the front door and bundled the boxes in the van, then managed to drag the desk out and lock up, and here I am." He looked terribly shaken.

"Oh! 'It's' still there!" I gasped.

What would happen with the new folk – would 'it' still be there for them?

I had learned that when this large estate of bungalows had been built it was on land that had been woods, called 'Mad Bess Woods', where it was believed a poor mad soul had roamed.

We had Christmas parties with our Christian friends, but also there were 'others' who were less than desirable and some drinking and card playing took place. We played at Fortune Telling and, yes, I was backsliding and stepping on dangerous ground. Looking back on this it is best to pull down the blinds. Whatever went on, whatever it was, it began revealing itself to me, to my horror.

Mam and Dad had come down to holiday with us when we first noticed. Victor was doing a house clearance, which he had begun as part of his business. It was near Northolt, at a large house, where he had already removed certain items he thought he could sell. This was when he thought a Junk Shop would be a good idea, having left the little lock up shop when we moved from Ruislip.

After he had stacked his van with items, he arrived home and carried an old stone, Victorian table round the back, which I was thrilled about. It looked good on our patio; a grand table for our garden and Mam and I admired it.

Then, laughing, Victor came dancing in with a large, very ugly mask on his head. It was horrible to look at and Mam shrieked, "Oh! Get it off, and out of here, you should not have fetched it in here! Bad luck if it remains! Oh, get it out now!" She was terribly upset.

Suddenly Victor couldn't breathe. He snatched it off his head and rushed out to the front, got into his car and drove off. It was really alarming. It appeared Victor had felt something strange and he was going back to the old house. He slung the old mask over the hedge into the garden there and drove home again.

Mam insisted, if we kept the stone table, we should hose it down with cold water, which is what I did. I still wanted the table, even though she warned it could 'hold' something. A few days later they left for Yorkshire, and the mask was never mentioned again.

Life went on. Then, from our Church, a young man came along. He was a believer, and from Barbados. He asked if he could lodge with us because he had nowhere permanent for his home. His name was Lionel and he moved in.

Belinda's nursery was a nice room for him, so we moved her into a little annexe, which she loved. I had painted it lemon, raspberry and Kingfisher blue, and Victor had made her a large set of shelves for her toys and books. It was so bright and cosy. We had no idea we would be especially glad we had moved her out of the nursery.

Lionel had been with us a week or two when I felt 'something' affecting me as I knelt in prayer in our lovely, spacious sitting room. 'It' seemed to be behind me, preventing me from praying. Lionel came into the kitchen and said he couldn't sleep; he was getting a feeling of 'something' or other kind of 'gliding' over his face and it was disturbing him.

What was it? We all spoke to our pastor and he and his wife, an elder and ourselves decided to pray in the nursery. The pastor told us afterwards he was nearly knocked clean off the bed where he was sitting in prayer.

After this, 'it' seemed to go, until one night I saw a tall black shape over by our bedroom window. It didn't remain for long. In the few seconds I took turning over to tell Victor 'it' disappeared. That seemed to be the end of it, but I was nervous.

By this time Lionel was courting Theresa, a lovely girl, and they did get married. They had found a house of their own so, when Lionel moved out, we returned Belinda to the larger nursery again, keeping the annexe for her toys. She had a funny little cough which never seemed to go, but all was well otherwise.

CHAPTER 36

Working In Quarantine Kennels

I felt I would like to earn a bit of extra cash and looked in the paper to see if there were any jobs I might fancy. I didn't want housework and was interested to see a job for a young woman wanted as kennel maid – enquire Uxbridge Quarantine Kennels – Mr Dougal.

I wrote giving my age, which must have been early forties because Belinda was coming up for five years old. I explained some of my experiences from the past and received the request that I should go for an interview immediately. He was happy to take me on and, dressed in trousers etc., I set off, with the family joking, "Don't end up on the vet's table!"

On my second day at the very large kennels, housing thirty dogs and eight cats all quarantined for six months, I was given the job of introducing myself to each animal and then, at intervals, letting the poor creatures out into three concrete yards, one dog to a yard in rotation.

Jack was a strong, noisy bull terrier belonging to an Australian. His owner never once came to see him while I was there. Poor fellow just lay in his cage, bored stiff. He proved too strong for me, leaping up and grabbing my trousers and his teeth sank into my leg. I crept into the vet's office.

Mr Dougal looked at me with such an expression, then took me to Hillingdon hospital for an injection. I never fully lived it down. He used to call me and the other kennel maid 'blackguards' – nice!

Golden Labrador was in the famous
film "The Incredible Journey". was sent
to Kennels where I worked, because
of exema. The Alsation was "Peace" belonged
to a Japanese. Kept him in Qearantine
18 months before coming to collect him

A beautiful German Shepherd called Peace, owned by a young Japanese fellow, had been left there for nine months. She was so lovely, except for the day I took Belinda in with me and she was in the yard with Peace. For some reason the dog began nipping Belinda. I'm not sure why unless it was jealousy on the dog's part.

One day she got away from me and ran around the house grounds. I was petrified I would lose her as I saw her grabbing at the grass frantically.

I loved the beautiful Dalmatian, Duke. The old fellow was stone deaf and gentle.

There was a little imp called Mac, a Dachshund who loved me. He was visited every week by his master, an American Air Force captain. I got friendly with this man and his young son, Buddy. So much so that when I became pregnant and had to leave, Mac was brought to see me. He yelped in delight and flew into my arms, licking and bruising my lip in adoration.

Buddy met Belinda and came to her fifth birthday party dressed in red jacket and bow-tie. I wonder where they are now?

There was Ladybug, a 'Butterfly' dog; little, pretty, cocky, snappy, and yappy – I had to watch my ankles…

I hated it when dogs were brought in for destruction. Mr Dougal injected them, then we'd walk them to a shed where they sank down and died. So upsetting. The dead dogs and cats were collected by a Kent lorry firm who loaded them on and carried them away. What happened after that I never asked, it was too distressing.

The other kennel maid, Sue, told me she'd slept with a hundred boys! She was only sixteen and the last time I saw her she was pregnant... She loved the dogs though. We were both to help with the surgery, but I had no training and I'm pretty sure Sue hadn't either, so when I was asked to give anaesthetic to a cat I overdosed it. Mr Dougal saw in time and was able to revive it.

I only fainted once, when he removed a cat's eye, and cried a couple of times when there were sad cases, like an old female cat having to have five stillborn kittens removed from her.

An old woman used to visit her spoilt white terrier, bringing in oranges for her. A dog's digestion can't cope with such fare, though they generally eat anything, so it was no surprise the dog messed all over her cage. Mr Dougal told her off (the woman, not the dog – she couldn't help it). Mad woman. We weren't happy either because the animal's bedding was old clothing, which we were supposed to wash every day in an old electric washer which never really worked properly. I got fed up with that.

My biggest fright was when a beautiful Belgian kitten came in for six months. The owner was rich and the head of a gang, and he'd refused to have his pet quarantined, so they had to enforce it. Mr Dougal was out seeing cases when the man came round, with a couple of henchmen, to remove the cat and I had to bolt the doors and get help. It was a scary experience I can tell you.

One morning I arrived at the kennels to find a big Alsatian where Jack the bull terrier had been (Jack was now reunited with his owner). The poor beast lay with a great swathe of skin ripped off and tyre marks showing. His name was Satan. He was in an awful state and I sat down and cried.

The old vet saved him though, and we helped with his operations. He would have scars for the rest of his life.

The dogs did bark at night and the worst barkers had their jaws bound up overnight. We hated that. Mr Dougal wasn't too kind but he was good at his work. He told us one day that he had been a medical student in hospital, wanting to go into surgery. He went on to tell us he couldn't stand some humans' behaviour.

What finished him was when an enormous woman came in for bowel surgery, whilst he was still young. He was given the task of giving her an enema and she passed wind straight in his face then screamed with laughter, wobbling like a jelly. She thought it a huge joke – Mr Dougal did not, hence he turned to animals.

I had to assist lifting a large Labrador onto the operating table and I felt something 'pull away' inside. I hadn't known I was pregnant, and I was too ill to carry on. It was so sad having to leave that job. I lost the embryo, just as I lost three altogether over the years of trying. I wasn't meant to bear children, but at least we had Belinda.

Oh, I wish people could see the poor dogs pining away (one or two actually died). They would surely think twice about their supposedly 'beloved pets' and find a more humane solution.

Mr Dougal came looking for me to go back to work for him, some months later, but by then I had my pet shop. He has long passed away and the kennels gone.

CHAPTER 37

On The Stage

I made a lot of friends – an occasional boyfriend too in those earlier days, but nothing very lasting. I'd come home, still with my Tourette's symptoms, and was often ridiculed, which I never was at Glaisdale. Country folk were kinder. I learned to ignore the taunts, or get my own back, which I often did, and found it great to be on stage, with the youth drama group. I remember taking part in the play, *Six Wives of Calais*, and later I was Emily Brontë in another play.

Eventually I joined the 'Three Arts Club', in the Town Hall in Loftus, becoming more involved and taking part in a three act comedy play, *Fools Rush In*, written by Katherine Reback and Joan Taylor. In our next production I helped with the scenery. We performed the hilarious *Love in a Mist* and so many others. On one occasion I fell over a main cable and fused all the lights. Of course the audience roared with laughter and I didn't know if it was right or wrong to carry on speaking, but that's what I did when I could be heard again.

It was during the 1950s when Joan Littlewood's group came to perform a snatch of Shakespeare in Loftus Town Hall. They all stayed over in town and we were all asked if we would 'put up' the group. Would we! Wow! I was twenty-one and thrilled to bits that I had Robert Newton's daughter, Sally, sleeping in my bed. I kept her soap long after she had left – years in fact!

Joan Littlewood was a bit of a reprobate, as a famous

producer. What a thrill to meet her, and there were Jerry Raffles and George A. Cooper, who appeared in *Billy Liar*; George had played the father in that. Howard Goorney and Ewan MacColl as well (born James Henry Miller – we found him highly intellectual but a snob). All these famous people and I met every one of them.

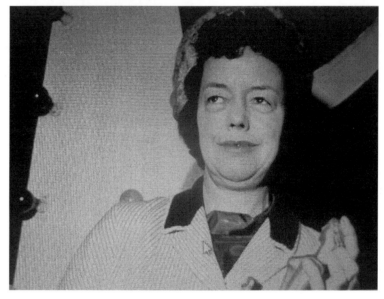

George stayed at Marion Lindsay's and was fascinated with 'real Yorkshire cheesecakes', made from curds.

We met Ewan's young ballerina wife and child. Later in life Ewan met Peggy Seeger, a folk singer. I believe his daughter sadly died.

He was a brilliant man. In the war he disguised himself as a hunchback and lived in the hills, I never found out why. He didn't like us singing down our noses like our hippie friends, who sang folk songs that way; he wanted us to sing from our diaphragms when we were in performance. As I had, and still have, trouble with my diaphragm muscles, it didn't really work for me, and he was rather rude to me.

Joan Littlewood invited our group to join hers on their teaching holiday, when we saw them again in Appleby, so six of us booked up with them in Whitby and had a great time in Appleby. Joan was a hard taskmistress – almost a bully. Two things stuck in my mind that she said to me. I had been out with my paint box and was late for one of our rehearsals, while in training.

Luckily I knew how to enter a room when late – I slid in quietly, keeping behind everyone, swiftly found an empty chair and gently sat, not speaking 'til addressed.

Joan stopped speaking and remarked, "You entered like a piece of thistledown."

I thought it was a lovely observation and was thrilled that this great producer had said it. Next day, when I had a small speaking part, only three words, referring to a part of the reading, I spoke clearly and she told me afterwards, "You haven't the team spirit, dear, stick to your painting." Probably she had watched me during other rehearsals, but it shattered my dream of becoming an actress; I was no good – that was that.

We were in one of Ewan's training sessions on how to stand when singing; he thought I was standing rather lazily and when I quietly informed him it was due to me being trapped under a car, and I couldn't help being lop-sided, there was no apology.

In the end, when I had been married about twenty-five years, I met with a group of housewives and we began a little travelling group, where I did monologues, or a 'Gert and Daisy' with friend Mollie. We were quite successful and had a lot of bookings.

At this time I, my husband Victor and daughter Belinda, were living in Malton, near Pickering. The ladies and I performed in many villages, between York and Scarborough, at Evergreens, charities, and the Womens' Institute etc. It became a decade of fun.

We kept a diary. When we were booked we often had no

idea what sort of conditions we'd be performing under. Sometimes no piano, even no toilets or refreshments, and the 'hall' could be large or nothing much more than a big shed.

There are a couple of amusing entries in that diary which I will allow to speak for themselves:

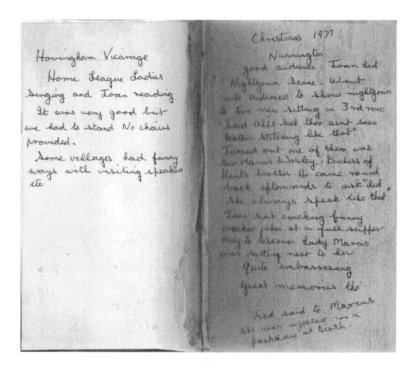

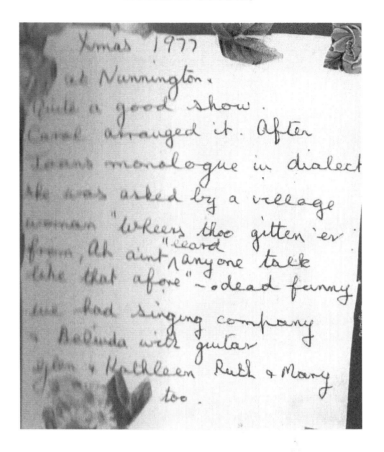

Xmas 1977 at Nunnington. Quite a good show. Carol arranged it. After Joan's monologue in dialect she was asked by a village woman "Wheers thoo gitten 'er "eeard" anyone talk frae, Ah aint like that afore" - o dead funny we had singing company & Belinda with guitar & Kathleen Ruth & Mary too.

Victor gave us transport in his furniture van, even in winter, with thick snow falling – very tricky driving. Eventually we had a troupe of youngsters travelling with us.

I was into my fifties, Mam and Dad were still alive and in their nineties, so a long time had gone by. Sadly Mam had Alzheimer's and it seemed I had lost her then; she forgot so much of my life and her worries fears and foibles.

CHAPTER 38

110 Cambridge Road, North Kilburn

Our first home was an awful tenement house in the slum area of North Kilburn. We had no money to speak of, though Victor kept up the dry cleaning for some time.

When he had his old motorbike with a box behind, I would sit in the box as we drove about and no-one could see me because there were no windows. The door was just on a hook and little did anyone know I was in there. Every time he started up to drive off the old bike issued a loud 'phee-ee'.

The other tenement occupants seemed weird; one poor little soul lived on the first floor (we were on the second floor). Her name was Julie, a Polish refugee, middle aged and unmarried as far as we knew. She had suffered at the hands of the Germans, in a prison camp, and we could often hear her screaming and thumping around in her room of a night.

There was a terrible smell as you came into the house and one day, as Victor was passing her open door, he decided to knock and ask her, "Julie, what's that dreadful stink?"

"Non smell. Non, non, no thing smells in this place."

"Julie!" bawled Victor. "It's coming from over there!" pointing towards her wardrobe.

On top of the wardrobe was a large cardboard box. As he was tall he lifted it down. "It's something in here," he croaked.

Julie screamed, "Leave! Leave!" and she ran at him but

Victor opened the box and found a dead, putrid cat. It had been Julie's pet and her poor brain hadn't worked sufficiently to have it buried properly.

Victor burnt joss-sticks all around, after getting rid of the rotting body – perhaps all Julie had left – and when we finally left that home we never knew what happened to Julie; she had no-one.

Another tenant, on the ground floor, was Mr Jensen, a Swedish gentleman who kept company with a common woman, Mrs Norris, whose Scottish husband was in prison. Mrs Norris lived on the top floor and was very clean.

One day Victor had left the main front door open while he carried in some chairs for our two rooms. She yelled at him, they rowed and she bit his hand, then she screamed at me and said she was a decent woman – at that point her top set of teeth fell out.

Was I in a Lunatic Asylum? What was I doing here after a life of fresh air, beautiful meadows and rolling hills? I had made my bed and I must lie on it.

When Mr Norris, the Scot, came home from prison there was another row. He jumped down the stairs, wearing only his comb's (combination underwear) to attack Victor.

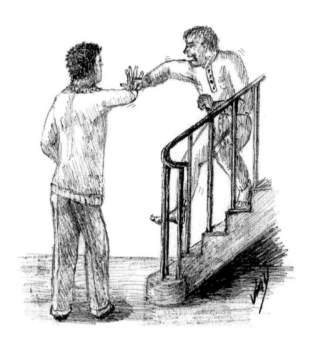

Things settled down for a while. We furnished the bigger of our two rooms very comfortably and tried to keep ourselves away from the others, but Mr Jensen had a small bedroom on our floor. As a result he saw me quite often and began asking me down to his sitting room for lemon tea, every day. I was polite and went, but got weary of it.

One night I had been out with friends and came back late. I discovered I'd forgotten my key and rang the first bell my finger landed on. Unfortunately it was Mr Jensen's and he hurried out to let me in then pushed me into the wall. I screamed and punched his face.

Victor heard and jumped over the bannisters, so Mr Jensen ran out to the pub, which was almost next door to us.

Victor took him to court. I was about collapsing and became a nervous wreck. Eventually the Judge asked the poor old, trembling bloke, "What did you do to this little woman?"

I suddenly felt sorry for the poor old guy and was glad when he was just let off with a warning, although the police were none too pleased. Next day he brought me a half dead bunch of Sweet Williams.

Victor found somewhere else for us to live and we never told Mam and Dad anything, so they never knew about it. Anyway the whole area of Cambridge Road houses were pulled down soon after, and a new estate built there.

CHAPTER 39

7 Colville Square

We moved to Colville square – just around the corner from Portobello Market; more tenement houses, but respectable and clean. A two-roomed flatlet, once again on the second floor, we overlooked an enclosed garden surrounded by trees.

The other tenants were pleasant and one of them had a flabby ginger cat. The young couple on the top floor had a Dalmatian named Bessie, a lovely natured dog. We became close friends with this young couple, Kirtle and Christoph, who were from Basle in Switzerland.

Next door to us was another Swiss, Willie, and in the next house along there was a posh lady with a poodle called Alexandra. She took him for his 'walkies' in the enclosed garden, calling "Alexandra!" in quite an upper class voice. Over the road, in another large house, a concert pianist practised the same music over and over again. It did get to me some days.

I spent a good deal of time down in the market, and made friends with a large lady behind the greengrocery stall. She would be drinking stout and offer me a drink. "'Ere, a drop o' this an' yer will liven up gel." She kept up her stall until into her eighties.

I really loved the market and we would often go up into Notting Hill Gate for a coffee and a snack.

Our two friends, Kirtle and Christoph, had their first baby, but sadly it was deformed and died a few days later. Kirtle went back to Switzerland; Christoph stayed behind to work, sometimes leaving Bessie with me.

I lost my first early pregnancy here too – I was ill for some time after.

When Christoph went back to Switzerland I was sorry to lose the companionship of Bessie. A year later I was sent a photograph of their second baby; a beautiful little girl.

Willie, after two years, was returning home as well, but before he went he said he would love to visit Yorkshire, on a farm, could I help? I contacted the Hogarth family, in Whitby, and he had a wonderful holiday there.

Months later he sent me a lovely pressed Edelweiss from Switzerland, which I still have in my scrap book. We took over Willie's room and were very comfortable by then. I used to walk around a lot, doing my shopping, and round the corner I dealt with a lovely little dairy.

Mummy and Daddy Scher used to visit and once Mam and Dad came down to stay, which was amazing.

The only notable incident, while living in Coleville Square, was on the morning after bonfire night, when we were all awakened by a loud explosion. Two young lads were out on the balcony and were messing about with some loose gunpowder, left in some used bangers. The amount they'd collected was enough to explode and blow one of the boys' hands off. Oh, how horrible.

CHAPTER 40

First 3-Bedroom Home – 99 The Fairway

Mam and Dad helped us to buy a lovely house in South Ruislip, where Victor took on a lock up shop. He was now into upholstery and carpet-laying and did very well.

Having furnished our new home we took on Toffee, a little brown whippet. We rescued her from a life of being left all day fastened to a washing line in the garden while her folk worked. Victor also bought me a black cat we named Mr Cinders – until one day 'he' produced a litter of four kittens, under our old gas fridge; then we dropped the 'Mr'… Our favourite was Dumbo, who had very large ears.

He was a pretty cat and such a darling; we always left our front room window open so he could climb in, leaving paw marks all down the wallpaper, only when we were at home of course.

We had been away on holiday, so had to put Cinders and the kittens in a cattery, Toffee the dog in kennels – when Cinders came back she and the kittens were riddled with fleas and we had a flea infestation. Anyone who knows what that is like won't be surprised that fleas were very quickly everywhere, even in our beds, and the next door neighbours suffered the same. Toffee had been clear but was soon scratching as well.

The Pest Control people told us there were flea larvae on the walls, and it dawned on me that two of the kittens might have died from the sheer number of fleas on their poor little bodies, although one of them was found with her jaws clamped around a small stick, we couldn't understand why. I can't recall her name but she was the first to go missing. Later we found Dumbo lying under the lilac tree and it was evident someone had choked him. We could prove nothing but there was a rather nasty French woman living nearby who hated cats...

I was so thick and green; I now know I should have gone back to the cattery and complained. God help any other cat owners who had used their 'services'.

We had to stop the local kids coming in with their dogs when the Pest Controllers scattered crystals all down our stairs, and on the floors in all our rooms. We lived and walked on these crystals for weeks until they evaporated, but people kept clear of us and we felt so unclean and ashamed. Eventually we gave the surviving two kittens away and Cinders mewed for them for days.

She lived until she was sixteen.

It put me in mind of that other flea episode, back when I was poultry farming in Scotland. We could only hope other people never suffered this pest. Luckily these were cat fleas and we didn't seem to get bitten, but we must have stunk of the crystals. I think there was camphor in them, which in turn reminded me of the sweets Granny had in her bedroom chest along with her mothballs.

Victor finally opened the little lock up shop, and when he came up with the idea of lodgers upstairs – again – I wasn't keen. We let to a young American airman and his wife. He turned out to be half Apache and was quite an unpleasant young chap; I felt very sorry for his wife.

We still trusted them, and stupidly went on holiday, taking Toffee with us, but leaving Cinders. When we came back we found they'd filled the house with family coming for a holiday... They went...

Another couple came; no children, and they seemed intelligent. He was a weather forecast broadcaster and his wife was deaf. I can't remember his name but he wasn't Michael Fish... They moved on eventually.

We applied again to the American Airbase and went a week or two before the doorbell rang. When I opened the door I saw a smart couple standing there in full uniform. I guessed African. I noticed they were officers, husband and wife. He spoke in a nice voice. "We understand you have rooms to let."

"Yes," I said simply, "come in."

The young woman put her hands together and gave thanks. They followed me upstairs and I showed them the small kitchen and the larger bed-sitting room. "We didn't think we would find anywhere, thank you. May we please take the rooms now?"

Victor came up and at once they were our new lodgers. Nobody had wanted them because of them being black. We were shocked. They were a good couple. The wife liked a drop of the 'auld' stuff and would get herself into a crazy mood; we'd just put her to bed if hubby was on duty.

They were with us for a few months, but her drinking got worse. Then orders came for them to move on – an order from the American Air Force. I would have liked my house back, but Victor decided he would carry on with having lodgers, so I guess I just put up with it in the end.

The next were two sergeants, Cliff and Mick. Mick was a short, dumpy bloke and lived on vodka. Cliff was more domesticated. He cleaned the rooms and tried to keep Mick in check but Mick began having 'DT's' – he couldn't keep off the drink and became unmanageable. Then we discovered Cliff had a prostitute hidden upstairs as well, who crept in and out without us knowing. We were being used and it had to end. Would Victor ever give up having blasted lodgers?

During the following year Victor found another little lock up shop, where he sold upholstery cottons, cards, pins etc. I used to go over to Northolt and look after the shop and we kept it going for about six months. Then a bungalow came up for sale in Hillingdon, which victor decided to view. Oh how weary I was getting of moving so many times.

CHAPTER 41

Norton-On-Derwent

When Victor and I moved back to live in the large village, Norton near Malton, we called a firm from there to take our furniture and deliver it. We drove up there together, with Belinda, Uncle Tom and a friend of his named John following behind, while Victor and I had the three dogs with us in the van, along with two Aylesbury ducks, Daisy and Dora.

Each time we stopped for refreshments we lifted out the crate so the two ducks could drink like the dogs. Other travellers thought it hilarious seeing and hearing two ducks pecking through the bars to get some grass, or sloshing their beaks in water and quacking.

It was dark when we arrived at the house, and no furniture yet. Luckily the previous owners had left an old bed, two big armchairs and there was a kettle. We had blankets and tea and some food with us so it wasn't too bad.

We let the dogs out into the garden, and rather stupidly the ducks as well, who quickly found the stream. I had no torch so going to find them was rather difficult and I walked down gingerly, calling them, only to find myself in water and, worryingly, no ducks. Luckily they appeared next morning.

Victor and I had the big bed, Belinda the floor in a sleeping bag, and the two chaps slept in the armchairs.

The furniture arrived late – they had had a puncture – well I wonder, they also liked a drink... They were two typical Yorkshire lads, and it seems not as experienced as they should be at their job. They'd had an accident with one of my antique dolls and an oil lamp, having packed them together. They also let my piano slide on the stairs which bust some beading and my china cabinet mirror was broken.

"Oh," said the older bloke, "it'll stick together."

"Oh no, not a glass mirror won't!" I exclaimed.

"Oh, you Londoners," he began.

"*Oh* no! It's a good job you aren't dealing with my mam, a true Yorkshire woman, and *so* am *I!*" He knocked a bit off the price. I was furious.

We found out they were local antique dealers and not always fair and square; we were never friends with them in all the seventeen years we lived in Norton-on-Derwent.

I first met the Diddecoys when we bought the big old house in Norton-on-Derwent. One morning the doorbell rang and I hurried down the long passage to open it. I was faced with a gipsy, selling pegs which didn't last long, but I bought some and off the old woman went.

This was the start of an association with the gipsy family, who had caravans in Pickering.

I was brought up with half gipsies in East Loftus; they were spotlessly clean and 'dressed to kill'. When the moon was full they often fought amongst themselves, but we never interfered.

Eventually my new associates were given an encampment in Malton. They then became regular callers. I bought pegs and lace, which Ivy measured by holding lengths from her nose to her outstretched fingertips. That was a yard, as used way before standardised measuring gauges.

I bought paper flowers made out of toilet rolls, gave her clothes and cups of tea, after she regularly told me, "A sup of tea has never touched me lips all day!" Finally I told her I'd bought so many of her pegs I'd go with her to sell mine. I can't remember if she ever laughed, or even smiled.

One winter she brought her daughter, Annie. It was bitter outside so I invited them in. They sat by my open range and Annie fell asleep with her head drooped in her basket of wares. Ivy cleaned my brass and began calling me Mother; then she told me Annie's young man was in prison.

She asked me to write him a letter, which I did as from Annie. I don't know if he ever got it or if he is still in prison; he was in for 'grievous bodily harm'.

CHAPTER 42

The Raggle Taggle Gipsies

By the time Belinda was ten years old, we got letters from Mam and Dad, telling us they really needed help so, after many discussions, Victor and I decided we would move north again, and bought a large old house, which needed work, for £4,500. (In later years we sold it for £10,000. Today's prices would be £200,000 and goodness knows how many hundreds plus.)

We had been married thirty years at this time, and I joined the Women's Institute. That's when Mollie became a new friend, and joined myself, Mary, Rachel, and Kathleen, along with other housewives, to become a group of speakers, invited to different Women's institutes around the York area.

We spoke on quite a few different subjects, my speciality becoming herbs and wild flowers. Mary sang songs about flowers and other things, in her contralto voice. She was very popular.

Kathleen and Rachel joined us when we wrote short playlets, and we formed a Victorian Group. It was wonderful to dress up and enter pageants and carnivals. We displayed at garden fêtes, taking along our dolls, teddies and children's toys which we all collected.

When we sold up and moved again, to the junk shop, it was some months before we began to have customers, and that's when old Ivy turned up again.

She sat in the back yard, still begging and selling. I asked her where the clothes were that I'd given her and why she wasn't wearing them. She told me they were wet – she would have sold them no doubt. She was around for many years after that and, when we had another bad winter, I took an old duvet down to Ivy's camp. It was a bit of a blizzard, not too bad but enough to wet and it was intensely cold. I found them sat outside around a bonfire, one young member in just a cotton frock. It was then I realised they didn't know they were cold. What a hard life they lived.

Dolls display at Mr Puffet's Garden Party, Pockley 1979. My first attempt at displaying.

Dolls display at Mr Puffet's Garden Party, Pockley 1979. My first attempt at displaying.

When we moved again, to Whitby, I sometimes visited back in Malton and saw Ivy in the town for the last time. She asked me if I had any old clothes. I had to explain that I lived in Whitby now, so I wouldn't have any old clothes if I was there visiting for the day.

I haven't seen her for years now; she may be dead, but I have great respect for my memories of her and her family; they never stole from me and I remember them with some affection. We became quite well known, as a troupe, over quite a large area between York and Scarborough. We even dressed like gypsies and 'camped' as a living display, with an authentic caravan.

On one occasion though it was touch and go whether we would be allowed in at first because we looked so convincingly like the real thing.

It's intriguing to think, with my maiden name being Dickens, that there might have been a connection with Charles Dickens. We began to do readings from his works, quite unaware of this possibility at the time, until I gave a talk about Charles Dickens during one show. I didn't mention that my maiden name was Dickens so it was odd, when I'd just finished giving the forty-five minute talk, that a strange, elderly lady, came up to me and asked, "Are you a descendant of Charles Dickens? I'm sure you could be."

I love the feeling that I could be. I have often wondered about it since, but will probably never find out. There were lines of Dickens in my family, and many similar interests, especially with my dad. Who knows?

CHAPTER 43

T'awd Codgers

We often used to drive over the vast moors to Whitby, and then on the coast road to Easington to see Aunt Winnie. She belonged to an Over 60s Club. One night they had been to the club and the group of entertainers never turned up.

Aunt Winnie said, "We had nowt to do and we were bored."

They were all disappointed and it set me thinking; what if we got a little group together so we could be 'filler ins'? As I had acted before I was married, and while I was in Ruislip I had joined the Townswomen's Guild and played parts in sketches, including writing a short panto myself; I mentioned it to Belinda. She was interested and offered to play her guitar, and sing in her lovely voice. Two of her friends would recite poems.

Glen was another young man who had joined us. He had a same sex partner and was a very pleasant and amusing guy. He came along to the Norton and Malton Carnival with us, in 1977, and he and I did a 'Mr and Mrs', as on the TV quiz show.

He pushed me over three miles in a wheelchair, which caused a laugh. It was a good carnival. We didn't win a place but we both looked good in our Edwardian outfits. It was a three mile walk around Norton, as a part of the carnival, which I can't say I enjoyed as I was coming up for sixty years old.

A bloke, in a 'Master of the Hounds' costume, followed us around and said to Glen, "Can't she shut up talking?" He was too thick to realise it was a part of the act. It was a fine August day and it was hot, so we were pretty tired.

That was when I met Gayther (soft 'th'), a jolly little lady who ran a children's theatre group in Malton. Belinda joined them and Gayther then introduced adults and put on pantomimes, bringing back old memories for me. Of course I joined as well.

I had already asked Mrs Gayther Coates (as she was known at this time – she married again later on) to see if she was interested, and she was thinking about it.

Eventually, after about a year, we became 'T'Awd Codgers' and there were about eight or nine of us. We talked and talked and finally we sent news around about our first show. We were quite excited; we'd be entertaining crowds at the Rydale Folk Museum, in Castleton, at the edge of the moors.

It was August 1975. Gayther brought some of her little troupe, 'Derwent School of Dancing', with her and we were to perform on an old farm cart – short sketches from Charles Dickens in a Yorkshire dialect.

Our first snippet was from *David Copperfield*, his birth and the visit of his Great Aunt, Miss Trotwood. Our Salvation

Army friend was Miss Trotwood, I was Pegotty and John Hutchinson, a member of 'York Dickens Society', played Dr Chillip. He had a very quiet voice and didn't seem able to ad-lib as we did, though he looked very effective in his Dickens suit and top hat.

As Pegotty in the sketch, I announced, "The child is a boy." And Molly, as Betsy, whacked me so hard the wax flowers on her bonnet flew off into the audience.

Gayther then played Mrs Squeers from *Nicholas Nickleby*, re-enacting the giving of brimstone and treacle to the 'poor boys'. Her bustle fell out as she bent to the task and we had to re-fit it.

The tape-recorder wouldn't work, and too much noise came from 'backstage'; we concluded it was a bit of a wash out, but it didn't put us off. We received £5.

For some reason John fell out with us and didn't join us again after this.

We would all crowd into Victor's furniture van, without seats or seatbelts, and our second show was my first playlet, *Granny and the Cheque*. This was performed at Leavening Women's Institute in November 1975.

Molly played Granny and forgot some of her lines; a friend, Dorothy, only had one line but she forgot that too. Gayther was the main comic part and acted it too well; falling down in a faint so convincingly she lost her mob-cap and tried to recover it in front of the audience.

I forgot myself and asked, "What are you doing Gayther?"

"Looking for me cap," she answered, getting a laugh for the wrong reason.

The play went off fairly well in spite of this and we were paid £2.50 for petrol. We were served a good W.I. supper afterwards, so it was worth going.

Next there was Filey, in December 1975. It was the Deaf and Dumb Society at Filey seaside town and we mimed nursery rhymes. We wore Victorian costumes and held up posters giving the title of each nursery rhyme we performed.

Joan, Gayther, Molly, Dorothy and Mary.

Three ladies, sitting in the front seats, were blind as well as deaf and dumb, so we walked over and placed balloons into their hands. They weren't aware of what was going on – so very sad. We sang with keyboard music, but they didn't really hear us, though some did have hearing aids. However, there were nine of us that night and we all felt it was worthwhile. It made us think we should consider giving more of our time for disabled groups throughout the North Yorkshire villages.

Only three of us were free to give our performance at St. Peter's Church in Leavening; Molly, Ivy (semi-professional Music Hall singer), and myself.

The piano was out of tune to a certain degree, but Ivy coped well. Molly and I did our 'Gert and Daisy' duologue and, in one sketch, Molly misheard and entered in the wrong place with her lines.

Again I 'lost it' and said in a stage whisper, "You've come in ovver early."

"Oh, O.K." Molly turned to the audience. "A'll gan off and coom in agean!" and flounced out. The audience roared with laughter.

Christmas 1976 and we were invited back. One of Belinda's Salvation Army friends was with us, Duncan Bartlet, a very amusing young lad. Molly and I did our nightgown scene in original Victorian nighties but the audience was invited from West Riding and they didn't catch on to our North Yorkshire dialect.

We had to use the kitchen as our changing room, where the women were making supper. They had a coal fire lit, with a large fireguard surrounding it, my dress caught on that and a long thread pulled out as I walked through to the audience, all the way. A good supper was served.

When we returned to Filey, again for the blind folk in December 1976, we invited Malton Salvation Army along. We all described ourselves before we sang or recited poems, and the Salvation Army Officer told the Christmas story. Belinda sang and played her guitar, we did our 'Gert and Daisy', and the audience laughed and clapped. I loved this best of all, the privilege of being able to entertain disabled people.

Unfortunately we didn't do so well when we went to the Old Age Pensioners, near Leavening. Molly and I did our nightgown scene and the audience chatted all the way through. We had to ask them would they be quiet. Two blokes were discussing their football pools and a young lad was rude. We were mad. We asked, would he like to come out and do a show on his own? We didn't go there again – too rude.

I had many parts, like Cinderella's godmother, a soothsayer fishwife, even Marley's ghost, all swathed in bandages with real chains around me. While waiting to go on a little dancer needed to pee. She couldn't go because she had to be in a dance routine. She peed on my padded feet. Poor bairn still had to go on to dance, dripping.

I fell over my chains as I entered. The audience laughed thinking it was meant, but it wasn't.

I was the crocodile in *Peter Pan*, for which I took ages making the croc's head and claws but finally I managed. One night I bruised my knees crawling onto the stage, as the pirates whopped me with their 'swords'. I was sore. I should have had more sense, at sixty, however on the last night I grabbed a pirate's bare foot and pulled him down. He went with a crash and a yell.

It was Gayther's son, David, and it caused a big laugh from the crowd but I don't think David was too pleased.

I also played 'front of curtain', called 'Tabs', while scenes were being changed, doing monologues etc.

At this point I met Mollie, a Salvation Army lass, and through her I joined the Salvation Army. Belinda followed, became a junior soldier and played the timbrels. At seventeen she became a senior soldier, joined the band and played cornet. She also sang in the 'Songsters', becoming very well-known and popular. She planned to go to the Army College, and by the time she was nineteen had met Morgan, also a Salvationist and cornet player.

By twenty they were married. Our life had by now become a little calmer and I settled into a more relaxed state. I did miss the pantomimes though.

To train as officers for Salvation Army

Two Norton women have been accepted for training as Salvation Army officers.

They are Christine Beales (24), of 45 Langley Drive, and Belinda Scher (20), of 48a Commercial Street.

Both have been members of the Malton Corps for many years and first attended the citadel in Wood Street, Norton, as children. They are senior soldiers, and as corps cadet guardian, Miss Beales has special responsibility for young members, while Miss Scher is a Sunday school teacher.

It is the first time in about five years that the Malton Corps has had candidates accepted. They will start their two-year course at the Army training college in London next September.

Miss Beales, whose mother

CHRISTINE BEALES

and older sister are uniformed Salvationists, is a nurse at Malton Hospital, where she has worked for 3½ years. She trained at Scarborough Hospital.

Miss Scher's parents, Mr and Mrs Victor Scher, are corps adherents. She works in York as

a secretary with a firm of accountants.

Both are former pupils of Norton School and are members of the corps band. Miss Beales plays baritone and Miss Scher solo cornet and guitar.

Lieut. Maurice Hunt, commanding officer at Malton, was delighted they had been chosen to be among about 150 people attending the college in Denmark Hill, London, later this year. The average age of candidates used to be between 18 and 20, but now it was about 24.

Miss Beales made up her mind to become a full-time member about three years ago but first wanted to gain experience in a job other than the Salvation Army. "I think my nursing will come in useful, but I don't necessarily see myself

BELINDA SCHER

continuing it when I have completed my studies.

"I have not really thought about where I want to serve, and I shall be happy to go wherever I am sent, but I would like to go abroad for a while."

Miss Scher said she would prefer to stay in England.

Never Slept A Wink   Dialect

Ah'm not feeling over grand Ah've had an awful night,
Ah 'avent slept a wink at all, thats why Ah'm not so bright.
Fost thing Ah 'ad to do was mek sure t'fire was out.
An' then collect our Grannys cats, Ah really 'ad to shout
yan cat went out Ah shut the door, collected up another.
Two left in Ah shoved them out, yan cam back, what an awful bother
Ah oppened t'door, two cam streaking in, Ah was raving mad.
Then Ah trapped my little toe, it was hurting bad.
An just as Ah was climbing t'stairs, Granny gave out a roar.
(She'd gone on up to get to bed, about an hour before.)
"Wind up t'clock our Racheal, thoo forgets it, <u>do it now</u>."
Tawd Grandfather clock stands at top of t'stairs
Ah 'ate t'awd thing anyhow.
Ah pulled t'chains over &rd t'awd weights fell off wi' a bang,
"What's going on", our Mabel screamed, Ah 'eard an awful clang.
Ah stamped on t'landing, got into bed, when Granny yelled again
"Racheal, wheres me medicine, its getting late, its nearly 'alf past ten.
By this time Ah'd 'ad enough, Ah 'ad an aching 'ead.
"Now settle down all on you, Ah'm off to sleep." Ah said.
But suddenly Ah awoke, Ah smelt something burn on t'landing
"Whats bonning", shouts our Henry, Ah saw him there, just standing
Thoo's bonning cries our Mabel "Hes lit a fag he'll set 'oose
on fire, We'll all be bont to bits"
"Fetch fire brigade for goodness sake," She was 'aving fits.
Hot ash had set his jammas smouldering, Ah went and
Got some watter, chucked it ower his jacket,
By gom what a night, how much more
"Ah'm sick of all this racket"
Ah'v come downstairs to try an sleep
But theres a cock bod perched next door, it crows.
Ah've already said if it wont shut up
Int casserole it goes.

(Re-write before Lazer copy)

CHAPTER 44

4 Mayfield Place, Whitby

We moved to 4 Mayfield Place, when Victor became ill with heart trouble at sixty-two. A whole bunch of Pentecostals helped us with the move, piling all our worldly goods into a van which had had goodness knows what in the way of agricultural stuff in it, from animals to farm machinery. All was well until I got to Whitby and was waiting in the new house ready to give them all a cup of tea when they arrived.

I popped outside for something and heard the front door bang behind me. I was shut out in the cold of a late autumn with no keys to get back in. I went next door and knocked on the door. "I'm ever so sorry," I said, "but I've just locked myself out."

"Oh, you'd better come in and sit down then; I'll get a cup of tea."

Mary and Sid Jones became quite good friends, although Mary seemed a little strange sometimes, I think the loss of her daughter at age twenty had 'got to her'. Sid made me some little wooden houses which I still use as Christmas decorations, creating a little 'Hamlet' along my windowsill.

The people of the close were all quiet except one, poor Hilda. She was a widow whose husband had been a captain in the Merchant Navy. She was what the locals would call 'barmy'. She grumbled at everything, but she took a shine to Victor and came to us for help. Eventually she had a breakdown some months after we last spoke to her and it ended with her screaming and collapsing. We took her to hospital and stayed with her 'til she was settled in. Sadly she passed away in a nursing home.

Mac by Aunties Fire, and Kays Rug and a ball

I had given up the stage and our life wasn't so busy. Instead I spent my time writing poetry, which I had published, and attended the Salvation Army there. We had no pets either – the house felt empty but I had made friends with someone called Kay. Who had a little Westie she'd named Mac.

He was a darling and he would come with me when we went 'sticking'. I'd get a bagful of sticks from the woods to take home for our coal fire. This was our last home with a coal-fire; we'd had a lovely log-burning fire in our home in Norton-on-Derwent – I do so miss open fires and the magical kingdoms you could create within the glowing depths.

CHAPTER 45

More Of Our Houses

It was an interesting time in my life, having a pet shop. We had rabbits and guinea pigs, and bred white mice, hamsters and gerbils.

We took in unwanted animals, birds and a scraggy kitten. A woman brought in three budgies with deformed feet and we stood their cage on the counter in the shop. Soon an older woman came in and asked if she could buy them. Her son was deformed and he would love looking after those poor little birds.

I think we just gave them to her.

We took in Daisy and Dora, two Aylesbury ducks which were being kept in a shed with just a small bowl of water; we kept them ourselves for some years. We called the scraggy kitten 'Scrag End' and he took to sleeping with four puppies we had brought to us; there was also a half Alsatian/Collie puppy, called Jason. He stayed with us but the other four were sold.

Jason became ours and got on well with Bunty, and there was also a Doberman named 'Dorcas'. She was a weak little runt when we first had her but she was quite handsome as she grew older.

Then we were given 'Donald', who was another Aylesbury duck, and the folk next door had three geese; they didn't want any more, so we took them in too.

Victor had been doing church work for the little Pentecostal Church where we worshipped in Hayes End, and he supplied Bibles, texts, loudspeakers and so on. He decided not to 'let on' he was running two businesses, when we had the pet shop and junk business in tandem. We had quite a busy pet shop, which we simply called 'Pet Supplies', and eventually the junk side was phased out so the whole premises became a pet shop.

Joan and Jason, 1970.

It was devastating when the rabies scare came about in the sixties, coming from foxes and spreading over England. We didn't sell any more of our livestock, no-one wanted them and they had to be destroyed, apart from five Muscovy ducks, hens, and later a Mallard and a Khaki Runner duck. We also had a hamster called Florence, named after someone I knew – quite a menagerie. Sadly, the pet shop area was closed down so we went back to junk. We began selling second hand books as well. I was so sad.

It was then we decided to return to Yorkshire. We went house-hunting and were very impressed by a big Victorian house. It had belonged to the I. Anson family, originally from France and well known in the Malton area. Mr I. Anson owned a racehorse in Norton and, after his death, his sister-in-law and her daughter lived there.

Miss I. Anson was very beautiful as a young girl and dressed very elegantly, in a rather different style from the local women, and she used makeup. She was dubbed the 'painted lady', and when her mother passed away she became very lonely. Finally she wasn't seen for some time and, on investigating, she was found dead; she had fallen down the old cellar stairs.

The old 18th-century ballad 'Sweet Lass of Richmond Hill' was composed in Richmond, by Leonard McNally, music by James Hook. Leonard McNally was Miss I. Anson's ancestor, and I have now met a descendant of hers, a young curate from the old church, 'St. Martin of Le Tours' in Chelsfield, Kent; an admirable speaker.

We wished our parents could visit us more often, but when they did Mam said one day that she had a very sad feeling come over her, from the atmosphere in the house – Miss I. Anson I would presume – everywhere Mam went it was the same. Every house I have ever known has shown its atmosphere; is it me I wonder? I hope not.

CHAPTER 46

Malton, Number 23

And 'Mrs Junk Shop'

I was sad when our pet shop closed. We had two different Aylesbury ducks, Tinga and Tucker, which we took with us when we moved to our new home, at 23 Welham road, Norton, Malton; a fine old market town, along with the 'Scrag End' kitten, Jason, Bunty and Dorcas, the dogs. Cinders stayed with our very good friends across the road.

We had bought this six bedroomed, three bathroomed house, and it had three large downstairs rooms and over 200ft of garden with a trout stream at the bottom.

It took six months to finally settle. Belinda soon settled into school, made many friends and became a star pupil. She took up the guitar, had singing lessons, and soon was in a children's theatre group.

I was in my element, furnishing our 'mansion' and gardening. Soon I was back at the old game and kept chickens again; ducks too, in addition to the two surviving Aylesbury ducks, we'd brought with us. We had seven Muscovies, two Mallards and a little brown Chinese Runner duck. Ducks really need streams or ponds, so having the trout stream was wonderful for them.

For a while we had Gertrude, a large white goose we were given by a young villager, but she was killing my pullets and had to go.

Victor said we could take in lodgers and soon we were full up with stable lads. Malton is famous for racing and all around us there were racing stables, so that's where we advertised our rooms. Every day we would see all the race horses being exercised around the area – lovely animals but highly strung.

We kept the master bedroom and Belinda had the larger attic room. The stable lads were two or three to a room and we never had a dull moment. It was busy work. Victor cooked breakfast, I cooked in the evening, hired a 'daily' and we did all the beds and housework; the laundry was sent out.

We had trouble with one young lad, Mervin. He had been in trouble before he became a stable lad. His grandmother brought him up, his dad was a waster and he didn't seem to have his mother around either. We found he was 'light fingered' and he was finally caught by the police. He had been in a phone box with a large spanner, drunk, and he'd also peed in the phone box.

The police came to us that night and I had to go with them, in their Panda car, to speak for him. There I found three policemen questioning him, shouting at Mervin, as though that would improve his rather 'comical' answers. The coppers were trying not to laugh.

"Who do you live with at home, in Leeds?"

"My grandmother."

"What's her name?"

"Daisy."

"Daisy?"

"Yes, Daisy."

"What do you do?"

"I'm a stable lad."

"Where are you staying?"

"At hers." Pointing at me.

"What were you going to do with the spanner?"

"Dunno."

"What did you pee in the phone box for?"

"Dunno."

Nobody got anywhere with him. He was however warned and he confessed that he'd broken into our meter as well.

One policeman had been watching Mervin and one day asked if he could conceal himself in our upstairs room, so as to listen to the conversations Mervin had with the other stable lads. He laid his ear to the floor but was none the wiser. Oh what a gay life...

One of our Christian friends tried to take Mervin over, wanting to teach him better, but in the end he cleared off back to Leeds. Our friend was disappointed; he wanted to help Mervin.

Another of the older lodgers used to drink, and peed his bed. Victor stood the mattress up to see if it would dry beside his bed, because we didn't have a spare. Denny, the lad who had soiled it, came home from work and raged, "Did you have to stick it up by the wall like a bleeding Rembrandt painting!" He peed in the wardrobe – he had to go.

One day we found a squashed banana in Richard's bed when we came to change it. He was a jockey and had fallen asleep while eating it. Then there was the Irish lad, Patrick, who often came in drunk, and undressed himself as he staggered upstairs. He was warned, but we had had enough.

We decided we'd be better with long distance drivers, and we were, for a while, especially in winter – 'til one came to me once or twice and asked if I knew if there were any good women around. I told Belinda's friends one night, without thinking, and it turned out one of them, Gil, was a 'gay'. He borrowed some girly clothes and nylons and waited for our sexy lorry driver, enticing him for a date. The driver never came for an overnight stay again... So it went on.

The worst lodger was a transvestite – I won't tell what we came across in his bed... he was our last lodger, when we finally gave up the idea of lodgers.

One of our pet chickens used to come in of a night and roost on the downstairs toilet. This man went in and sat on it one night; we all nearly died laughing. The chicken wasn't hurt, just a bit shocked.

I had a row with Victor about payment. I took the transvestite's hand and told him to get out. He did, but before he went he threw pickled beetroot over the bedroom floor and turned on all the taps.

Who wants to be a landlady? Oh, not I!

CHAPTER 47

Another Move

Victor's temper was fraying and he decided we would sell up. He found a small, empty shop with a cottage and orchard. I was fifty-nine by now; Bunty and Dorcas were no more and were buried in the garden. I didn't want to leave Bunty behind and, as she was buried in a metal suitcase, I dug her up to take with us to be buried in the new garden. I lifted the lid of the suitcase and Bunty still looked quite presentable, poor love.

About six weeks after we moved, as I was getting into bed, I suddenly saw Bunty sitting there and I reached out and touched her. It was very real, but then she was gone, though not from my memory.

In the meantime Belinda had been wanting a cat and we heard someone had a cat with kittens. She went to see them and came back with two tabbies, Pinkle Purr and Solomon Grundy.

A semi wild Persian-type cat had adopted us, and we named her 'Little Ash'. She got on well with Pinkle and Solomon and produced four kittens later on. It was something of a miracle she ended up living for sixteen years, as you will see. I'm not sure what I felt when Victor opened the shop selling second hand furniture and loads of junk. He'd go to auction sales and buy up job lots, lined the shop with shelves and sorted all the stuff, filled the window and called the shop 'Little Bazaar'.

Little Bazaar and Morgan's old car, Eynsford. We were going to let the shop out after Victor retired, but we decided to sell and move to Whitby. Photo shows the whole frontage.

It made us a living but I was known as 'Mrs Junk Shop'. My life may have been hectic but there was never a dull moment with Victor.

When we had half settled into the shop, as we thought after renting it for a couple of years, it suddenly showed up trouble – and we were buying it!

Victor brought home a large old second-hand sideboard and in the middle room of the shop, no more than a barn, the sideboard was set down – the legs promptly sank through the floorboards with a crunch.

We had the whole floor taken up and underneath were fungi, like large mushrooms. It smelt terrible. This had to be done straight away and we called in the joiners. They laid the new floorboards and departed. For two days we didn't see two of the three cats we'd had – Little Ash, our half wild cat, and Pinkle Purr.

Pinkle Purr was our nosey cat. He was into all kinds of places and when Solomon Grundy stood outside the back door of the shop mewing I began to realise the other two must have been buried under the new boards.

Victor bawled and rowed but in the end he tore up some lengths of the new boards and out staggered two horribly soiled cats; their eyes and teeth filled with earth. Thank goodness Solomon had known. The poor things would have died a dreadful death. How Ash and Pinkle survived I don't know.

Victor was quiet about it and I could only be thankful they were safe after all.

Ash gave birth to her kits, lying in amongst the doll's furniture in a big open-fronted cabinet. What a cosy picture she made with her family – real life tenants!

Apart from a wasp nest in the shop office there was no more bother there, but oh my goodness – the cottage!

The cottage was falling to bits. First of all the outside toilet, and in the awful scullery it was infested with ants, just thousands of them running everywhere; mice infested the kitchen area and the walls needed repair and decorating; the sitting room fireplace needed to be taken out and replaced, the floor redoing and we couldn't get furniture up the narrow staircase.

We found a 'coffin hole' in the kitchen ceiling and the

upstairs bedroom ceiling had all the wooden slats parting and wind and rain was coming through. I tried to hide the fact from Victor, but we had no money left. The old woman who'd owned it hadn't cared; she'd had a lodger in there regardless of the open ceiling.

There were no proper windows in the big bedroom, until Victor had the wall knocked out and two windows added. Whole walls had to be re-plastered because they were covered in asbestos, which had to be removed for safety reasons of course. I became ill and Victor called the doctor.

He was disgusted at the state of the cottage. "Couldn't you have got your wife a decent place?" he asked Victor.

After two years Victor had managed to afford re-lining three rooms with special boards, which looked like oak panels, and finally a new stone fireplace – a log-burning fire with a copper canopy fitted – it was smart and decent at last!

The partition to the stairs was altered so furniture went up more easily. I had worked hard and had a full garden of herbs and flowers, the orchard was tidied and a proper chicken run added, so more chickens. We also had a duck we named Yak.

One of the neighbours, a long-distance driver, had been given a duck-egg, which sat for two days on his dashboard in the lorry. When he asked had I a broody hen I was able to say 'yes' and put the egg under her. She hatched out a duck, but its wings were permanently stuck out; he couldn't fold them up at all – he was a Concorde of a duck! Yak became a wonderful pet and followed me around. He loved Jason and, when he found him lying asleep, would waddle up and begin to peck his teeth.

Sadly Yak pined away and died while I was away in East Loftus looking after Mam and Dad.

We had many friends come and spend holidays with us and we showed them around the beautiful countryside; Malton, Pickering and outlying villages, Castle Howard, various museums and of course York.

After about four years Victor took over an old cobbler's shop, owned by a very elderly lady in Norton on Derwent, in the high street. We joined an Elim chapel before I became a member of the Salvation Army.

We sold the big house and moved into the shop premises. It had a flat and shop parlour-cum-kitchen, an outside loo, and orchard; more importantly no lodgers! Victor wanted the shop more than anything, and we were there for seventeen years; the longest we'd stayed anywhere. It was an interesting life.

Then Victor had to retire. A heart attack forced him to give up, but he also had leg ulcers and bronchial asthma.

After our seventeen years in Norton on Derwent with all our junk, in the old shop and cottage, we were off again, this time over the moors and far away to Whitby, to a comfy little house in Mayfield Place.

I was very sad to leave; I really had enjoyed my life in Malton. Now I was back to where I had been as a child.

We had a pleasant time in Whitby. Where there were regular carnivals. Belinda by now had married Morgan, a young Salvation Army officer, and moved to Kent. Isabel was her first born, then Leila followed. After about two years along came Daniel and six years later Joseph. All the while we were visiting them and they were visiting us.

This is when Victor decided we would have no more pets, no animals at all, and that was something I missed dreadfully. I don't know how I managed without them, especially as there were also no children and no Belinda around, except during holiday times when they would come up to visit us.

In the meantime we were looking after my parents, who were failing, and now in their nineties. Even though Victor had poor health he could still drive. Mam and Dad were still in their old house in Loftus. They had finally paid off the £500 it had cost them during the 1920s. It was a sad day when they had to go into a home in Saltburn.

The most memorable of Mam's words, for me, was when I had made her laugh over something or other (and she did laugh – a wonderful laugh – I can hear it still), she said, "Ah wish ah could put your face in my pocket, so every now and then ah could bring it out and look at it!" Only a mother could say that, and she smiled a great big smile as she looked at me. A photograph would have completely spoiled the wonder of what she said, it meant the whole world to me and was the most wonderful thing anybody had ever said to me.

She was ninety-eight when she died in 1995. Dad had been gone since 1993 – he was ninety-three, same as the year.

CHAPTER 48

The Salvation Army And The Methodists

In Whitby we lived a quieter life without pets, and I gave up all stage performances, joining the newly formed Salvation Army Corps and meeting many pleasant Christian friends. I also joined other small fellowships. Any poems I wrote were mainly for the Salvation Army meetings there and I spent a lot of time in our back garden.

I loved the Sunday marches. We followed the band and there is something amazing about marching along singing, behind the Salvation Army band. Victor and I remained adherents for over thirty years. They didn't have an altar or candles, like the Church of England and not many people went to their meetings, so didn't know much about what happened there. They weren't talked about much.

Christmas time in the Army Citadel was wonderful. It meant a big tree and a little nativity scene, plus the usual nativity play by the children – always hilarious.

One year a little lad tried to climb into the manger to be Jesus, and Mary and an angel had a scrap about who should hold 'Baby Jesus'.

The biggest scream we heard about, from another Church Nativity play, was Joseph knocking at the inn door asking for a bed.

The nine-year-old 'innkeeper' called out, "There's no room here!"

"Well we have nowhere to sleep so's Mary can have Jesus."

The innkeeper ad-libbed, "Well I can't help that, it's not my fault!"

"Neither is it my fault either!" shouted Joseph.

I think Jesus must often chuckle at Christmas time.

I loved the autumn celebrations too. The wonderful Harvest Supper, when the hall would be full with folks filing in who never came at any other time. The wonderful, rousing Harvest hymns, the lovely, crusty pies with thick beefy fillings, and the apple pies to follow. That is some dream supper.

The Methodists are also known for their 'good sings'. Before the Salvation Army came back to the area we used to go to the Methodist Chapel. A nice little group of friendly people ran it and we had different ministers preaching on Sundays. A particularly memorable time was the year we went to a 'Daffodil Rally' in spring, at Robin Hood's Bay Methodists.

Their chapel was filled with gold. Every nook, cranny, table and shelf was ablaze with beautiful daffodils, narcissi and jonquils. Oh, so lovely, brought by Methodists from all local areas, each with a scripture to read, or poem or song to represent their group.

Then of course there was the Tea; absolutely 'out of this world'. It is interesting that at one time dancing was not encouraged, in most religious groups, so it was unusual, on rejoining the Salvation Army, that we were all celebrating the harvest time with a Barn Dance.

Two Salvation Army ladies (both Majors, rather large and very jolly), popped in. They had come up from their Citadel in Portobello Market, to look at Whitby and to walk around saying quiet prayers, and as they saw our church open they walked straight in. They explained that the younger one had

had an amazing dream about sheep and steps, near the sea.

Of course Whitby is known for steps. One hundred and ninety-nine steps up to the old Abbey and St. Hilda's church, high up overlooking the town. Norma had been told about it by Pat, who had lived in Whitby as a child; all the steps around town, and sheep grazing on the steep hills. They believed it was a sign.

It was just outside of a year when they were back in Whitby with the old Whitby Salvation Army flag and the use of a hall, gathering a congregation. It was a great blessing for Whitby. The Methodists kept in touch through the years and we were sad to leave. We still kept in touch with our Methodist friends when we joined the Salvation Army again.

CHAPTER 49

The Lollipop Man

Victor and I drove over the moors or round by the coast road in his van, to visit Mam and Dad as often as we could; it was a shorter journey than from Malton, but the snowfalls in winter around Whitby could be really bad, and made crossing the moors pretty hazardous, so we had some hair-raising journeys I can tell you.

On one occasion, during the winter, we were almost blown off 'Blakely Ridge' on the way to Castleton, over and down into the ravine, but Victor managed to keep us on the road somehow, with our hearts in our mouths.

Another year some thoughtless children built a big snowman on top of 'Blue Bank' into the 'Sleights'. We skidded to avoid it and hoped no-one would get killed. How I wished the stupid brats could have been punished, putting peoples' lives in such danger. Blue Bank is treacherous enough in winter-time without adding this extra hazard.

Blizzards were the worst, even by the coast, and the area was so hilly 1" in 3" was normal.

Victor became a Lollipop man on the school crossing, although he didn't really have the temperament for it. With him being so large they couldn't find a cap and boots to fit. It got into the local papers – it was a bit of a scream though. He was not popular with drivers – he was very severe, but the kids loved him and when he left, at the age of 70, the school kids gave him a poster with the picture of him as a lollipop-man and all their signatures on it. He was very proud of that.

said I will be doing myself out of a job but what matters most is the safety of the children'

Victor Scher

Lollipop man calls for crossing

WHITBY lollipop man Victor Scher is calling for a pedestrian crossing at Whitby's controversial Mayfield Road junction – even though it might put him out of work.

Since starting work on the school crossing patrol in Mayfield Road earlier this year Mr Scher has been appalled at the number of motorists who ignore him, putting the lives of youngsters using the crossing at risk as well as the dangers of the junction itself.

"I have been a driver for over 40 years, and have never seen such unsafe traffic lights," he told the Whitby Gazette, pointing out that 9 streams of traffic in all converged on the junction.

"As a driver coming over the new bridge and turning right to go down to the Railway, after passing the stop/go sign I can not tell if the lights have changed to make it safe to turn right.

"As a pedestrian crossing from Caedmon Fields to the Fishburn side of the new bridge there is no light for a pedestrian to see. The same applies when crossing over Waterstead Lane."

His main concern however is the safety of children going to school.

He is on duty each morning - when, he says, the traffic is particularly busy - and again in the afternoon to see youngsters from Airy Hill, St Hilda's, and, unofficially, Caedmon Schools safely across the road, and has already been moved once, further up Mayfield Road away from the junction in a bid for greater safety.

He has had to report a number of drivers who have failed to stop - among them mothers with children in the cars - even when he is in the middle of the road with his stop sign displayed and hand raised.

And many drivers who do stop set off with he is still in the road - unaware that children might be running down the pavement to try to make it across before Mr Scher if off the road.

"My being in the road gives the youngsters a false sense of security. Many of them, instead of waiting till they reach me just run off the pavement as soon as they see me in the road, and no matter how many times you tell them, within a couple of days they are doing it again," he said.

And many older children, cross the road elsewhere - these would be more likely to use a zebra or pelican crossing, he feels.

"People have told me that by campaigning for a crossing I will be doing myself out of a job," he added. "But I don't mind that - what matters most is the safety of the children."

Report by Angela Cook

THE scene at the Mayfield junction after a Ford Cortina, driven by Whitby man Gary Jason Lloyd, knocked down one of the sets of traffic lights last week. The lights, which continued to operate while pointing skywards, were repaired on Wednesday afternoon. Police said no-one was injured in the single vehicle accident.

● Whitby Town Mayor, Councillor Maurice Hatton, raised the matter at Tuesday's meeting of the Town Council and moved that the council support Mr Scher by writing to the County Council, asking the County Surveyor to look into the possibility of installing a pedestrian crossing at the junction.

... and the council agrees

Nothing untoward really happened, until the day we were over in Loftus taking Dad shopping (Mam was going into Alzheimer's by then and he did most things now). Victor was crossing the Market Place when a car, swerving to avoid another car, came skidding across the market, hitting Victor's legs and throwing him up so his head came down and hit the bonnet.

He became very ill and never really recovered. It was our worst time.

We stayed in Whitby for nine years and I really hated having no dogs or cats; the house seemed a bit dead. You could say this was almost a boring life; we found it too hilly and the sea winds just about killed us both. We didn't consider moving until after Mam and Dad died, however, and then we moved down South, to be near Belinda and Morgan in Kent.

It was sad leaving good friends behind, though we visited them now and then, but Victor never got much better after the accident, even with family helping down in Kent, and he passed away in 2008.

I think he was happiest when we had our little junk shop, over in Malton. Life had to go on regardless but it had been a long haul. I remember he never really liked going on holidays, so it was a triumph when he finally agreed to go abroad. Only to Holland, but we had known two lovely Dutch families for some years, going over there three times in all, which was a bonus, and they came to us too. Those were happy times.

CHAPTER 50

Just A Dream

I've always had dreams of a small cottage away in the country. Even now, after a somewhat hectic life, could I do without a TV, a phone, neighbours, gas and electricity? Not at my age, no, but there was such a place.

It may still be there, very out of the way down in a deep valley in Yorkshire. How often I had looked down at the ruins of a tiny abandoned cottage in Horcum Hole and imagined what could have been done today, especially with Calor gas.

The nearest civilisation was a pub. Saltersgate pub halfway up Saltersgate Bank; very dicey in the winter with open moors stretching for miles around, and at the top a plantation leading out to fields of sheep, with here and there an isolated farm. Quite treacherous in storms and high winds.

There in Horcum Hole, though, high winds might not prevail. Snow storms would pretty well cover it in with packed snow perhaps, so you wouldn't even know the remains were there; maybe once a shepherd's dwelling. Across the valley ran a stream so water would not be such a problem.

The legend goes that once upon a time a giant and his wife lived at Saltersgate and, after a disagreement one day, the giant became so angry at his wife he madly dug out a massive hole to throw the earth at her. He missed his wife and all the rubble ended up at Guisborough as a big hill, known as Roseberry Topping, which I have climbed in my younger days.

Sometimes in autumn, when passing Horcum Hole, a mist would be hanging over it – very ghostly but interesting to see; a strange kind of beauty.

How old Saltersgate pub is I can't recall. I felt I could always go there, had I lived in the Hole, for friends and comfort; there would be plenty of food there. Of course there is a legend about the pub as well. The peat fire had never gone out. It was always glowing and always replenished faithfully, because the story was if it ever did go out the Devil would come down the chimney. I remember my uncle from Glaisdale taking me to see it and I was fascinated.

During the war a group of sailors, on leave, were drinking there. A very mean, cocky sailor decided he would pee on the fire and put it out. I think it would take more than that to quench such a fire, and I hope he got his just desserts for even trying. What an abominable man! Quite typical though...

I have never had my dream home and never will now. I wonder why no-one else ever thought about rebuilding that little cottage, it would be a lovely holiday home. The valley is full of weeping willows now, and cattle roam around peacefully.

I had a walk there one day with two friends and their dog.
There were cows with new-born calves and still the old white
bull was there grazing. He lifted his head and stared. I was
nervous but my friends weren't so we carried on walking,
leaving the big bull behind us. To our amazement, and my
horror, there he was in front of us, still glaring as we got to
the path.

I told my friends, "You carry on, I'm climbing under the
barbed wire and I'm out of here!" so I made it up the slope.
Luckily we were all unharmed as we got out and looked back,
relieved to leave him and his family to their own devices.

CHAPTER 51

52 Cherry Tree Court

We had lived in Mayfield Place for nine years when we decided to move back down South to Kent. We took a flat in Sidcup, not far from Belinda, Morgan, and family, but I will always miss the Yorkshire Moors and long to go back; that last farewell has been the saddest thing for me.

The flat belonged to a Turkish doctor who had moved to a new practice in the Midlands.

Although property had risen a lot in price, this flat was, we were told, still 'cheap' at £75,000 – a big difference from the £4,500 we paid for that six-bedroomed 'mansion' all those years ago.

It was quite pleasant even though it was near Sidcup Station. Soon we saw wildlife in profusion, which surprised me greatly. Foxes breeding along the railway embankment, hedgehogs, frilled newts, grey squirrels and also brown rats, but the birds were so diverse; green and lesser spotted woodpeckers, robins, hedge sparrows, blue– coal– and great-tits, blackcaps, all different finches, including greenfinches, as well as the more usual grey doves, woodpigeons, crows and magpies. There were yellow sulphur butterflies, tortoise-shells, whites, browns and tiny blues, as well as moths and bats, though not so many bees. The trees were just as diverse, with holly, wild cherry, limes, beeches, etc. Amazing.

A Chinese family had been renting it and had left it clean, with some furniture they left behind, along with kitchenware, which we used. Before them there had been an English couple living there, who had been abroad on holiday; as they were getting out of the taxi, on their return, the wife stumbled onto the forecourt and died.

Victor somewhat merry....
Hall Place . 2007

We didn't know about this when we first saw two expensive wreaths appear on the grass. I first saw them when returning home and thought one of our near neighbours had died. The wreaths arrived every year at the same time and we never saw who put them there. We later discovered it was her husband, daughter, and children who had asked permission of the neighbour to leave the wreaths, and she had never told us about it.

One year there was a bereavement upstairs; Dennis and Sylvie were a jolly cockney couple, so it was sad when Dennis died. We moved the wreaths out of sight for her sake.

We spent at least four years fighting an unpleasant builder, who unfortunately had bought the embankment from the railway company to build fourteen four-storey flats. We all fought hard and at least the work had not gone ahead after seven years. I hope he can never ever build there – any flats would be under the same threat as the Station House, which eventually began slipping away and has now been completely removed. The embankment is not safe for building. He had begun chopping trees down, but was prevented from continuing the devastation.

In the meantime Victor and I had been attending the local Salvation Army and, at one of their lunch clubs, heard a speaker from 'Mind in Bexley', an organisation to help the disabled and those suffering mental health problems. We were at a loss as to how to fill our days in and decided to go along to 'Mind in Bexley' to see what was on offer. They gave therapy classes and also counselling, which was what we needed because we were lonely, even though we went to Salvation Army lunches, Home League and coffee mornings.

Having joined 'Mind in Bexley' we then met two wonderful people who became our very close friends. Through their kindness we became members of Bexley Council for the unemployed, having asked if we, as pensioners, could join up with their group, lunch clubs and other activities. We really enjoyed belonging to such a friendly group and were members for seven years.

We went to Mind twice a week, joining the art classes and afternoon quizzes; there were trips to the seaside as well so we both found ourselves very busy.

I also joined 'Centre-pieces' art class, in Crayford, which was an outlet for my painting and creative picture-making.

Victor became very ill with deep thrombosis ulcers and had a serious operation. He finally became housebound and died soon after. A few months later Mollie, our little neighbour opposite, died.

I moved out to live with Belinda and family, and Morgan's ninety-year-old father also came up, from Portsmouth, moving into my old flat. One evening Belinda could get no answer, when she called on him, and let herself in. She found him lying in the kitchen, dead. What a shock.

The younger neighbour, to the left; an energetic bird-watcher, was also found dead in his flat. I had no wish to go back there. It has now been my privilege to live in a dear little annexe.

CHAPTER 52

My First Grandchild

Isabel was Belinda's first born. She and Morgan had discussed it and decided there would be no babies for the first two years… it was a few months later when Belinda rang one morning and I knew what she was going to say. I'd just been down to Kent visiting them and I'd noticed something different about her.

"Oh yes, I know," I said when she told me she was pregnant.

"Are you an old witch?" she laughed. "How did you know?"

"Ah well," I answered. "There you are."

She had a difficult time of it, poor girl, all through her waiting time, but I was shocked when she had a caesarean. Victor and I visited when Isabel was nine days old, a beautiful little girl already. I was so glad she was to have that name, and I liked her second name, Gwendoline, too.

Both were very happy with their first child, and of course we grandparents were too. Morgan's parents were to be known as Grandma and Grandpa, which fitted them very well, and we were plain Granny and Granddad, which was right for us too.

Isabel was a bright, beautiful child, and she loved visiting us in Yorkshire and going to the Army Citadel with me. She didn't want to go back home when the time came because she wanted to stay and "sing with Granny".

As she grew up she could certainly sing. She joined 'Brits' drama college in Croydon and would have gone far, but she changed her mind.

CHAPTER 53

The Snow Walk

While Victor and I were still living in Whitby one Christmas, Morgan and Belinda brought Isabel, Leila, Daniel, and six-month-old Joseph up to visit for the week.

It had snowed heavily and everywhere certainly looked very much the Dickensian Christmas. I decided to take them out over Caedmon Fields with a three-coloured torch to shine over the snow. It looked magical.

Did the kids love it? No, they moaned they were freezing. Well Daniel was wearing wellies without any socks; of course he'd be cold. They rolled down a little bank where the snow was packed thick and all laughed for a bit, but then they began to whine so, disappointedly, I said, "Oh, city kids! Come on then, let's go back."

I was enjoying the enchantment of the different colours sweeping across the whiteness; sometimes green, which was eerie, sometimes red which was even more weird, but then there was yellow which turned everything Midas gold.

That night I was to babysit while Morgan took Belinda out. I seem to remember they were going to the pictures and Victor went with them. I don't like the big screens so volunteered my babysitting services.

The girls behaved but not Daniel. He argued and yelled he wasn't going to bed and I cajoled and promised treats to no avail. Eventually I grabbed him by his pyjamas and hauled him upstairs, still yelling, with his legs dangling. "Right!" I said. "Stay up there until your mam and dad are back, and then you're for it!"

On one occasion we let Isabel stay with my mam and dad. She was six and excited about it, but we had to bring Leila back with us because Mam couldn't manage two children. "By gum," she remarked, "she's got summat off, that one; ah couldn't 'ave done wi' two on 'em at t'same tahm!"

Belinda wasn't keen on the idea; she never did like either of them out of her sight.

I can't remember what Isabel had done but I was told Mam had chased her up Tweed Street with a stick – not that she would have used it. I remember Sarah, a woman at the end house with a family of eleven, having to go out on dark nights armed with a stick rounding up all her youngest kids and her old man. "Ay oop!" neighbours would say. "Awd Sarah's off roundin' 'em up agean!"

Mam had Isabel for ten days – I think never again…

CHAPTER 54

The Miracle Man

Looking back over the decades I have one main regret, that I didn't spend more time with Dad, being his companion not just a daughter.

He was a brilliant man and should have gone further but, gifted as he was, he was humble and happy in his little terraced house with Mam.

Donald was eight years old when an uncle bought him a child's box of 'magic' tricks. The 'conjuror' was born as he taught himself to manipulate things with greater and greater deftness, entertaining relatives at parties.

By the time he was married he was semi-professional, performing at parties, dinners, weddings and on stage, both locally and further afield, like 'The Globe' at Stockton. Here he performed amongst names like Max Jaffa, and a young, ambitious Paul Daniels, whom Dad helped starting out before he became so famous.

Paul (Ted) Daniels visiting Dad at Loftus, 3 Glenfield Terrace, 1980s.

Dad was a member of the I.B.M. (International Brotherhood of Magicians), and in later years 'Merlin'. If he had lived another seven years, beyond the ninety-three when he died, he would have become 'Excalibur' on his hundredth birthday.

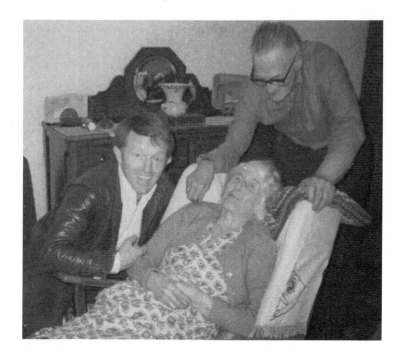

I always had a big birthday party in our back yard every year. It was in June and all the kids loved it: cakes being baked in a hat; rainbow streamers coming out of Dad's mouth; the magic words 'Hey Presto!', 'Like So!', 'Abracadabra!'; cards disappearing under your nose and appearing again out of someone's hair; eggs out of your ears; confetti; balloons being burst to reveal a gift inside and so on and so on.

He travelled to magic conventions, was a founder member of Middlesbrough Magic Circle of Magicians and was the first man in town to make a 'Cat's Whiskers' radio, which he would let the local men listen to when the racing programmes were on, opening the kitchen window for the chaps to come down the back yard and listen.

At the age of twenty-one he bought a second hand violin and taught himself to play. He was a great player and, with Mam playing the piano they spent happy hours duetting at weekends, playing wonderful music. During the summer they would open the sitting room windows so their music was heard better by the local 'oldies' sitting on the seat opposite. They loved it.

Dad was an artist. His pen and ink sketches were very professional, and he used water colours to great effect, giving them as wedding gifts amongst friends and relatives.

He taught me to draw and paint, an abiding joy for me ever since, and he taught me to read and write at four-and-a-half years old. He taught shorthand and typing at night school and was a great maths wizard.

Although his first job, at 'Skinningrove Iron and Steel Works' was 'office boy', at seventeen, he very soon became an accountant and, as the years went on, Senior Accountant. He was there until he was sixty-eight years old.

Oh, what a wonderful man. May I meet him again one happy day to tell him how proud I was of my 'Miracle Man'.

with Mr. Johnny Mac, who came second in the trophy competition.

And while there, he was able to teach some new tricks to an American expert who came over to lecture.

Mr. Dickens' favourite . . . . mental telepathy tricks.

His ambition after 45 years' performing . . . to do magic for another 45 years.

In a name

A STOCKTON colleague, picking up the details of a swimming gala, was stopping successful competitors after they had received their certificates and asking them their names.

One youngster, when asked his name, replied smartly "It's Alfred Dumais, sir."

"Ah, that's an unusual name. I'd better check it. How is it spelt?"

And just as smartly came another reply . . . .

"A-L-F-R-E-D."

FRIDAY, DECEMBER 28th, 1962.

Top magic

THERE was at least one occasion when Mr. Donald Dickens, of Glenfield-terrace, Loftus, walked ten miles through anonymity to entertain at Christmas parties in the dales.

To show how good he is considered today, he would also have to carry a trophy—that which Middlesbrough Circle of Magicians has awarded him as the most versatile magician of the year.

Mr. Dickens has won the trophy in competition with 14 other magicians. To gain it, he attended nine meetings (which involved him in a couple of hundred miles of travel) and he performed 35 tricks, ranging from children's effects to mind reading. He also used coins, cards, dice, rope, thread, liquids, magazines and lots more . . . but not a single rabbit.

Jovial Mr. Dickens, who was once in hospital after a road accident, and despite his injuries complained because he was put in a separate ward, and there was no one around to enjoy his tricks, recently attended a convention of the International Brotherhood of Magicians at Harrogate along

with Mr. Johnny Mac, who came second in the trophy competition.

And while there, he was able to teach some new tricks to an American expert who came over to lecture.

Mr. Dickens' favourite . . . mental telepathy tricks.

His ambition after 45 years' performing . . . to do magic for another 45 years.

AROUND THE SOCIETIES

MIDDLESBROUGH CIRCLE OF MAGICIANS: At our last meeting, Past President and Hon. Life Member Donald Dickens performed dozens of his favourite effects for us (writes a correspondent). Members were enthralled for nearly two hours. Donald has been a magician for fifty years and younger members will always be grateful to him for his generosity in passing on, so willingly, the fruits of his knowledge. Donald can always be relied on to show us something new and this time was no exception. It would not be practical to describe every effect performed but some of the highlights follow. Donald opened by tearing pieces out of a folded newspaper which, when opened, had a very artistic design torn in it and the words "Middlesbrough Circle of Magicians nice set of chaps"; the applause which followed this trick proved that members were in agreement with Donald's sentiments. A cut and restored skipping rope came next and experienced magicians we may be, but this one had us baffled. Donald followed this with a version of the Nudist Pack which can be handed out at the finish for examination. The next trick similar to the six card repeat, used ten cards and the patter was on the lines of "Ten Little Nigger Boys." This one had us all laughing and as Donald said it was grand practice for sleight-of-hand. Supreme's "Skatty Rattles" was next in his programme and I think one or two orders will be rushed to Supreme unless I'm very much mistaken. Donald shook us all with a prediction effect using Jumbo cards. A spectator was asked to shuffle a pack of cards under a silk scarf, three cards were chosen at random and returned in the pack. It was shown that these cards matched three Jumbo cards which had been in full view all night. Donald showed us the workings of this trick and we all marvelled at its ingenuity. At the end of a grand evening a well deserved vote of thanks was proposed by Mr. Graham Hood and members showed their appreciation to Donald in the usual way.

Mr. John A. Terry (right) with Donald the Magician entertaining pupils of Whitby Mount County Primary School at their Christmas party. From January 8th, Mr. Terry will be headmaster of the Airy Hill County Primary School.

ABOUT MAGICIANS

MAGICANA

By EDWARD GRAVES

At the express wish of the Brighton Corporation, the date of the 25th annual Convention of the I.B.M. British Ring has been altered to September 26 to 30, 1962.

Middlesbrough Circle of Magicians, who meet every second Monday and fourth Wednesday in the month, recently completed a competition of unusual kind. With versatility as its theme the members extended over nine meetings and the winner was Mr. Donald Dickens, who performed a forty-eight high tricks at them. Mr. Dickens, a fifty-year-old accountant, will receive his trophy at the Society's Annual Dinner adding twenty miles of travelling to the two hundred which accumulated during his odds and ends from home to the city as the only man who claims as well portunity to see ...tred differen[t]

MAGICIANS NOTICES

L. DAVENPORT & CO.,
25 NEW OXFORD STREET
LONDON W.C.1

SUMMER PRICE REDUCTIONS
SALE — SALE

	Usual price.	Now
Soft White Rope ...	4/6	3/6
Spring Flowers, pkt, 25 ...	1/8	1/6
Rigid Cig. Wand ...	2/6	1/6
Faked Thumb Spike ...	3/0	2/0
Wonder Table Runner ...	10/0	8/0
Cigarette Catching Fake ...	1/6	1/-
Cut Rope Routine ...	3/0	2/6
Tom Strip of paper ...	2/6	1/6
Jumping Bean ... doz.	2/0	1/0
Milk Fluid ...	2/6	1/6
Chinese Wax Box Pen. ...	1/0	9d.
Mouth Coils ...	3/0	2/0
Plastic Tumblers ...	1/6	1/0
Sponge Balls ...	6d.	4d.
Jap Silks, 12in. ...	3/6	2/6
Jap Silks, 9in. ...	2/6	1/6
Jap Silks, 18in. ...	5/0	3/6
Changing Bag ...	6/0	4/6
Handkerchief to Egg, silk ...	2/0	1/6
Handkf. to Egg ...	2/0	1/0
Elastic Egg ...	2/0	1/0
Golden Hook of Magic ...	1/6	9d.
Cork Balls ...	6d.	5d.
Stripper Pack Cards ...	7/6	5/0
Rough & Smooth Pack ...	7/6	5/0
Svengali Pack ...	7/6	5/0
Pack, Blue Black and Red Back ...	7/6	5/0
Forcing Pack, 52 alike ...	7/6	5/0
Metal Thumb Tip ...	2/6	1/0

Please add 6% to cover postage.
Write for latest lists.

WANTED, steg' illusion, immediately, Send full details, photographs and lowest price to Box 391, World's Fair, Oldham.

Out of the hat

DO THE GPO and the destruction of some letters by magic?

A letter received at Saltburn was addressed: "Donald Dickens, Esq. Magician." There wasn't another word on the envelope. The Post Office delivered it to the Evening Gazette, Middlesbrough, apparently knowing that there works Graham Reed, and he passed the letter along to Donald at his home in Glenfield Terrace, Loftus.

Where's the magic? They're both members of Middlesbrough Magic Circle.

SEPTEMBER 29, 1956

□   □   □   □   □

MIDDLESBROUGH CIRCLE OF MAGICIANS had a distinguished visitor at its meeting on September 18 in the Corporation Hotel, Middlesbrough. He was Doctor Zina E. Bennett from Detroit, U.S.A. Dr. Bennett has been in correspondence with members of the Middlesbrough Circle when it was first formed. Now they have made him an honorary member. Apart from an interesting tour of magical exercises is Mr. Tom Harris, of Derby. They were welcomed by Mr. D. Dickens, of Loftus, Vice-President of the Circle, who presided. The guests were thanked by Councillor J. N. Scott, of Thornaby, on behalf of the Circle.

□   □   □   □   □

Boro' magicians attend dinner

Headed by the president, Mr. Donald Dickens, members of the Middlesbrough Circle of Magicians with their wives and friends gathered at their third annual dinner at the Linthorpe Hotel, Middlesbrough, on Saturday. The vice-president, Mr. R. W. Thomas, welcomed the guests, and a made programme was given by Mr. and Mrs. Dickens.

The entertainment was opened by Mr. Peter Morrison, this year's winner of the Will Free Cup. He was followed by J. N. Scott, W. Johnny Mac, J. N. Scott, W. Ryder, and K. Johnson

---

FRIDAY, JUNE 28th, 1957.

Injured.—A car driven by Mr. Joseph Trillo, 57, High Street, was in collision with Mr. Donald Dickens, aged 50, 2, Glenfield Terrace, on Tuesday evening. Mr. Dickens, who is well known throughout Cleveland as a magician and entertainer under the name "Donald the Magician," was taken to Brotton Cottage Hospital with slight injuries, and was detained. The incident occurred at East Loftus.

CHAPTER 55

Trips Out

Morgan and I have often gone off on our own when Belinda is 'too busy'. For instance a holiday we had in Stokesley, Yorkshire, after Victor died.

We booked up at the Old Manor for six days. We were fascinated with the old house and thought it creepy. The landlady explained it had a history of strange happenings; people heard 'things', like singing coming from an inner room. "A lady haunts it," she said.

Both Morgan and I didn't like the long, winding stairs taking us up to the library and big sitting room; there was a 'presence'. Hanging in the sitting room was a painting of a daughter of the house, owned by a squire and his lady. Actually he was a duke in the 1700s.

The daughter was known to be spiteful, and wished to take over from her mother and be the Lady of the House. She was horrible to the poor servants. Her mother used to walk a couple of miles away from the house to the woods, in order to get away from her daughter. There is a stone shaped like a bench, and there she would sit and meditate. It is said she now haunts the house.

Looking at this painting, the daughter is standing, holding a bunch of flowers and staring into a mirror. As we looked at this reflection the face seemed to become a skull – it scared us – it actually changed shape. Morgan and I didn't like that room any more.

We walked the two miles to the stone bench the next day, wondering if we would 'see' the poor lady. It was a lovely walk, a bit rough but we photographed it. I couldn't climb up to the bench to sit on it, unfortunately, because of an arthritic hip. It was on the bankside.

We didn't feel any particular atmosphere there, only peace but, back at the Manor House, I really wasn't happy having to visit the bathroom at night when everybody was in bed – I don't think we will visit there again.

On another occasion, I think Victor's last trip with me in 2002, we both went off to drive over Gainsborough Way, along the beautiful moor road with gorse in full bloom on either side for four miles. We were hoping to visit a little village near Lingdale and I'd completely forgotten the turn off, having not been there for twenty years.

Owing to the fact that I have directional dyslexia I got directions wrong. Victor was not very patient about this so I said, "Stop the car and I'll go and ask at the little farm over there on the right."

"Well don't be long," he said.

I walked up to their yard door, which was open, and found the family sitting around their kitchen table having dinner. "Excuse me for interrupting," I began.

"Oh aye, what is it?" asked one of the men.

"We seem to have lost our way; I think we missed the turning for Moorgate."

"Oh, ah see – is thou from t'city then – doesn't ye 'ave a map?"

"Aye," I answered, "but I've read it wrong. I should have known – I was born up here!"

"Where?"

"East Loftus."

"Well, bah gum; that's a good 'un – ah'm from Loftus, t'market place!"

"Oh?" said I. "What's your name?"

"Gibson."

"Oh, the butcher!"

"Aye, yon at t'lads!"

"I knew Cyril then."

"An' tha's forgotten t'way – 'ave yer been away a long taam then?"

"Yes," I said, "over twenty years; I live in London now, my husband's from there."

"Bah, heck! What's thoo deein' married to a chap doon there for? A queer awd thing to 'ave tekken on!"

There were a few grins around the table and I was worrying about Victor, waiting back in the car. Mr Gibson finally gave me directions and I felt proper daft; I'm glad I didn't say who I was and hoped I wouldn't see them again.

We finally found our way and all was well..

CHAPTER 56

Forty Cats

An old tale goes round and round, in the area where I was born, about an old woman known as a crone. She lived in a tumbledown old cottage, away up in Grinkle. Grinkle was one of the most beautiful places you could wish to find.

The tale goes that she just seemed to appear from nowhere, found the old cottage and moved in. She tried to repair what she could, trying to keep warm. Where did she find water? Whose cottage had it been?

I am going back over ninety-odd years; who was she and where did she come from? Nobody ever seemed to know. Mam was a little lass when she first remembered seeing her, trudging the two or three miles to the nearest shops to pick up her provisions. How did she have money? How sad and lonely she must have been.

Maybe she worked at the farm, away up the fields? She must have belonged with somebody once. It must have been scary at night time, especially in winter, to be alone. Perhaps on lovely summer evenings she would sit outside listening to the birds' 'evensong'.

She had cats. One at first, maybe, wandered in from the nearby farm; it would have kittens and, as the years rolled by, as feral cats they would keep on multiplying. Did she give them milk or food? Did they come into the cottage? Did she have one as a special pet?

How people knew there were forty cats in the end I

wouldn't know. Did gamekeepers, or even poachers, know and how would they have counted them?

Somebody must have passed the time of day with her. She would hear no music or singing where she was. I don't even know if she could read and would have newspapers. Did she ever need a doctor? Mam never knew anything personal about her.

One year she stopped coming down for her provisions and someone decided to go and look for her at the old cottage, to see if she needed help. She could be ill.

All they found were the cats, hanging around mewling, spitting and snarling. No-one was in the cottage, where mouldy bread and an old jug of sour milk had been left on a rickety old table. The bed was only straw, and an old coat was hanging on a nail behind the door – she had disappeared as mysteriously as she'd arrived and was never seen again.

Nothing of her was ever found. The cats didn't look starving, in fact they looked well fed, but eventually they too disappeared. Where did they go?

I was once exploring in that woodland with friends. We came across about half a dozen building bricks and a piece of tiled hearth – was this where the old cottage had been?

Perhaps no-one will know. Now all the old folks are gone there is no-one left to tell the real tale, but it is still told today, as a ghost story. Maybe at night you can hear the cats mewling – if you are ever that way at night... I won't be. Did the cats know what happened to her?

CHAPTER 57

Visiting Yorkshire

I took the family to visit Loftus, to Hummersea, within walking distance. Coming to the edge of the double cliff was weird; you looked over the high point and there was a ledge below us where you could walk; this cliff was pretty high as well.

To get onto the beach you had to walk down hewn out rock steps and at the bottom stepped onto an expanse of coloured pebbles, sea shells and other fascinating objects, like fossils.

Wonderful treasures washed up; crab shells, purse-shaped egg cases with their curly extensions, cuttlefish bones, all sorts of driftwood and coloured seaweeds.

People from East Loftus would set off with picnics, during the holidays, with towels and bathing costumes. What an exciting time, climbing rocks, looking for rock pools, but being wary of thick mud that you could get stuck in and had to be helped out of; the pebbles, sand and mud were in patches from Whitby to Skinningrove. We didn't need to go on holidays when we had everything near at hand, like the moors, two and a half miles away, where we could picnic. We had a great life as kids.

Morgan and I would explore the beaches. Skinningrove was great and we went on a guided tour, down into the iron ore drift mine in the pitch black, where we heard an explosion which must have been to give us some idea of what it must have been like; it was a great museum, put together by a local miner. This was where my Great Grandfather Griffiths was an overseer – I was walking in his footsteps, learning how dreadful it must have been for young lads on their first days of mining, from the age of five years.

When the air became foul, for instance, they had to learn to hold the ponies' tails, because they could find the way, and the boys could walk out more easily. Rats would be about, often eating your food if you didn't secure it or eat it up. "Shut your bait trays lads!" was often heard; that's what they called their lunch tins. The ponies often went blind and had to be destroyed.

Morgan loved the moors and still does. We have driven miles and miles; they seem to go on forever. I remember finding some pieces of sandstone, just left in a heap, which I brought back to make a rockery. There were no restrictions in those days, as long as you didn't destroy property.

Women had 'Sticking' rights and would go off with sacks into the woods, to fill them with 'kin'lin'' for the fires.

We used to go brambling, in season; people tried to keep the best bramble bushes secret though. We'd carry 'Billy cans' and lined baskets. We even went 'Primrosing' as kids, tying them into little bunches and waving them at passing cars. Town visitors would stop and buy a bunch for tuppence (little more than today's 1p). There was 'Bluebelling' as well; gather as many as you liked. We wouldn't dream of being destructive though.

We looked forward to 'Conkering' in the autumn, picking up the shiniest, roundest ones and playing conkers with them. Bird-nesting was never right, though, it was a cruel thing to do, which I hated; I'm glad it's illegal nowadays.

CHAPTER 58

'Something'

Mam often 'saw' people coming down the yard, after I'd left home and she was sitting quietly with Dad. Once she saw a little man walk down our yard, stand at the back door and come to peer in the window, only to vanish.

I said I wondered if it was little Joe Morrison from the stables. The land our houses were built on had belonged to Joe. He buried fish bones there, and rotting herring, which had gone beyond being kippered. He went out with his horse and cart selling kippers and 'fresh 'errin'', buying up rabbit skins, for which he'd pay you a penny per skin. He'd then sell them on for curing, no doubt for making rabbit fur gloves etc.

He had been dead for years. He must have come back to look at the houses built there, or did he want his land back?

When I lived there, if I came in latish and Mam and Dad were in bed, I'd come in the front door, shout out it was me, lock the door and walk gropingly along to the kitchen doorway where I'd have to feel for the light switch, always with the sense 'someone' was going to snatch my hand. It was nerve-racking. There was 'something' in our house, I'm sure of it.

I still dream of going upstairs backwards – it's all queer.

Old Mrs Lacey, a fortune teller who told Mam and Aunt Winnie's fortunes, said there was a cloud around me. It could perhaps have been Granny Dickens who wanted to keep me safe. I believed she did but not now, I'm more inclined to think my safety is from answers to prayer.

CHAPTER 59

The Annexe – 4 Lapworth Close

After being left alone in the Sidcup Flat, I had been wondering what to do, and jumped at the chance when my Son-in-law invited me to go and live with them. What a relief. Victor had been gone a couple of months, Morgan was having his house enlarged and it was decided they would not just extend the back of the house, they would build an annexe.

I had tried to take out a loan to pay for the annexe but was refused due to my age, now over eighty, so we made an appointment with a solicitor so I could turn the flat over to Belinda. She, Morgan and I went together to do it legally, and she decided to 'take in' – no, not lodgers, tenants.

Which they did until Morgan's dad began to be ill and unable to do a lot of the usual things for himself. Morgan was driving up and down to Portsmouth to see him, and it made more sense that he should come up to be nearer where Morgan could help him. It worked out very satisfactorily. His heart was getting bad but he managed reasonably well.

Then Belinda made that shocking discovery. Dad had been out shopping and had been carrying bottles of milk and potatoes – he had collapsed and hit his face on the kitchen sink. It's believed he must have died instantly. Medics and police were called at once. We were all shattered.

Danny was as upset as Morgan was, because he had been staying with Grandpa, 'Gramps' as he called him, keeping him company.

242

I am very blessed to have my own little annexe – and no lodgers – only friends and family popping in and out most days. I was excited to move in and furnish it. My colour scheme throughout is linen white, gold, sage green and cherry.

I still have my old cottage piano, bought for me by Victor when we had our first home in Ruislip, standing next to my mam's pride and joy, her grand bookcase and china cabinet combined. It was a wedding gift for Mam and Dad in 1924.

The office where Dad worked as an accountant had raised £5 for them – a large white note and a lot of money in those days. The bookcase/cabinet cost just that, bought new, I could sell it for £200 now but I hope it never leaves our family.

I have Granny Robson's dining room chairs, newly upholstered in gold moquet. They are Edwardian and were matching with a chaise longue, grandmother and grandfather chairs, and a large pouffé, which I don't have.

We were not allowed to go into that parlour with shoes on, or grubby hands, they were for 'best'. When Gran died the chairs were split up. Mam had two and Aunt Winnie two, when they both died the four went to Belinda.

After five years they were falling to bits. Modern kids, you see, nothing lasts nowadays! They are my pride and joy, since I had them renovated.

I love my dad's 1950s desk; so useful to me, and all his fountain pens, school rulers, books and paintings. My kitchen is a little 'galley' kitchen with mugs and pottery jars for tea, sugar and so on set about on shelves. It looks cute; not much room but it's just right for me.

The piano, now where the desk used to be, with some of Joan's Art work

I have an all glass back porch, which is effectively my front door and lets the sun in. There I have Mam's old basket chair, which came from India, sent for by Granddad Dickens

244

for Mam and Dad's wedding day gift; it's about fallen to bits now. Also dog biscuits, bird food, geraniums and other plants, where Millie our Golden Labrador dog likes to sit. She also has a habit of dragging her bedding out into the garden on fine days, in front of our shed and veranda which we grandly call the 'High Chaparal'. She's very friendly and all my friends get a very warm greeting from her, she'll even bring a ball or something up to them, waving her whole body with enthusiasm, not just her tail. I have Mam and Dad's German striking clock and Victor's Westminster chiming clock, striking one against the other; it's great to hear them. Trouble is they lose time and I am for ever altering them and they end up chiming the wrong chimes at each quarter.

Millie will keep dragging her bedding outside.

Friends come each week for lunch, or coffee, or tea time, for which I am very grateful, and I am settled and happy. I'm never bored now, though I do become very tired and often drop to sleep in my chair.

I am still a Salvation Army adherent, and a member of two Baptist Church fellowships, also the Army Lunch Club and Evergreens. Besides MIND and all the other groups, there is also a new group, '4/Israel'.

Jay and Joan with Millie being silly.

Some Sunday mornings my neighbours take me to a village Mission Church and other times the big Methodist Church where we enjoy singing.

So, I am busy…

Annex building work.

Cliff Laying the first brick. Gran in Charge!

Now then Mr Elms, lay it right.

Annex in the snow. My bedroom on the left, sittingroom on the right and the main building set back a bit.

...paral' with Millie.